THE
DEATH PENALTY

OPPOSING VIEWPOINTS®

Diane Andrews Henningfeld, *Book Editor*

Bonnie Szumski, *Publisher*

Helen Cothran, *Managing Editor*

OPPOSING
VIEWPOINTS®
SERIES

GREENHAVEN PRESS

An imprint of Thomson Gale, a part of The Thomson Corporation

THOMSON

GALE

Detroit • New York • San Francisco • San Diego • New Haven, Conn.
Waterville, Maine • London • Munich

THOMSON

★

™

GALE

LIBRARY OF CONGRESS CATALOGING-IN-PUBLICATION DATA

The death penalty / Diane Andrews Henningfeld, book editor.
  p. cm. — (Opposing viewpoints series)
Includes bibliographical references and index.
ISBN 0-7377-2929-5 (lib. : alk. paper) — ISBN 0-7377-2930-9 (pbk. : alk. paper)
  1. Capital punishment. 2. Capital punishment—Moral and ethical aspects.
3. Capital punishment—United States. I. Henningfeld, Diane Andrews.
II. Opposing viewpoints series (Unnumbered)
HV8694.D3814 2006
364.66'0973—dc22   2005052743

Printed in the United States of America

"Congress shall make
no law...abridging the
freedom of speech, or of
the press."

First Amendment to the U.S. Constitution

The basic foundation of our democracy is the First
Amendment guarantee of freedom of expression.
The Opposing Viewpoints Series is dedicated to the
concept of this basic freedom and the idea that it is
more important to practice it than to enshrine it.

Contents

Chapter 4: Should the Death Penalty Be Reformed?

Why Consider Opposing Viewpoints?

"The only way in which a human being can make some approach to knowing the whole of a subject is by hearing what can be said about it by persons of every variety of opinion and studying all modes in which it can be looked at by every character of mind. No wise man ever acquired his wisdom in any mode but this."

John Stuart Mill

In our media-intensive culture it is not difficult to find differing opinions. Thousands of newspapers and magazines and dozens of radio and television talk shows resound with differing points of view. The difficulty lies in deciding which opinion to agree with and which "experts" seem the most credible. The more inundated we become with differing opinions and claims, the more essential it is to hone critical reading and thinking skills to evaluate these ideas. Opposing Viewpoints books address this problem directly by presenting stimulating debates that can be used to enhance and teach these skills. The varied opinions contained in each book examine many different aspects of a single issue. While examining these conveniently edited opposing views, readers can develop critical thinking skills such as the ability to compare and contrast authors' credibility, facts, argumentation styles, use of persuasive techniques, and other stylistic tools. In short, the Opposing Viewpoints Series is an ideal way to attain the higher-level thinking and reading skills so essential in a culture of diverse and contradictory opinions.

In addition to providing a tool for critical thinking, Opposing Viewpoints books challenge readers to question their own strongly held opinions and assumptions. Most people form their opinions on the basis of upbringing, peer pressure, and personal, cultural, or professional bias. By reading carefully balanced opposing views, readers must directly confront new ideas as well as the opinions of those with whom they disagree. This is not to simplistically argue that everyone who reads opposing views will—or should—change his or her opinion. Instead, the series enhances readers' understanding of their own views by encouraging confrontation with opposing ideas. Careful examination of others' views can lead to the readers' understanding of the logical inconsistencies in their own opinions, perspective on why they hold an opinion, and the consideration of the possibility that their opinion requires further evaluation.

Evaluating Other Opinions

To ensure that this type of examination occurs, Opposing Viewpoints books present all types of opinions. Prominent spokespeople on different sides of each issue as well as well-known professionals from many disciplines challenge the reader. An additional goal of the series is to provide a forum for other, less known, or even unpopular viewpoints. The opinion of an ordinary person who has had to make the decision to cut off life support from a terminally ill relative, for example, may be just as valuable and provide just as much insight as a medical ethicist's professional opinion. The editors have two additional purposes in including these less known views. One, the editors encourage readers to respect others' opinions—even when not enhanced by professional credibility. It is only by reading or listening to and objectively evaluating others' ideas that one can determine whether they are worthy of consideration. Two, the inclusion of such viewpoints encourages the important critical thinking skill of objectively evaluating an author's credentials and bias. This evaluation will illuminate an author's reasons for taking a particular stance on an issue and will aid in readers' evaluation of the author's ideas.

It is our hope that these books will give readers a deeper understanding of the issues debated and an appreciation of the complexity of even seemingly simple issues when good and honest people disagree. This awareness is particularly important in a democratic society such as ours in which people enter into public debate to determine the common good. Those with whom one disagrees should not be regarded as enemies but rather as people whose views deserve careful examination and may shed light on one's own.

Thomas Jefferson once said that "difference of opinion leads to inquiry, and inquiry to truth." Jefferson, a broadly educated man, argued that "if a nation expects to be ignorant and free . . . it expects what never was and never will be." As individuals and as a nation, it is imperative that we consider the opinions of others and examine them with skill and discernment. The Opposing Viewpoints Series is intended to help readers achieve this goal.

David L. Bender and Bruno Leone,
Founders

Introduction

"One possible reason for the increase in support of the death penalty is a declining belief that innocent people are being executed."

—Jeffrey M. Jones

Kirk Bloodsworth, an ex-marine with no criminal record, was accused of the 1984 rape and murder of a nine-year-old girl. His arrest came as the result of eyewitness testimony, although Bloodsworth argued vehemently that he was nowhere near the scene on the day of the crime. Despite several irregularities in court proceedings, Bloodsworth was convicted of murder in 1985 and sentenced to death. After nearly nine years on death row, Bloodsworth and his attorneys convinced the court to compare his DNA with that from semen found on the dead child's panties. The DNA did not match. After a second test in 1992, Kirk Bloodsworth became the first man in the United States to be exonerated from a capital crime based on DNA evidence.

Today, most Americans have heard of DNA technology. In an increasingly sophisticated process, scientists are able to compare the unique genetic signature found in biological material (such as skin scrapings, fingernails, saliva, or semen) left at a crime scene or on a victim to the DNA of a suspect. DNA testing has proven to be a powerful weapon. DNA technology, however, is a double-edged sword that both simplifies and complicates death penalty jurisprudence. In the hotly debated areas of justice, fairness, and public confidence, DNA technology both bolsters and undermines the death penalty system.

The promise of DNA technology is that executions of the wrongfully accused can be eliminated completely. Massachusetts Governor Mitt Romney, for example, believes that "advances in forensic science . . . have made it possible to adopt a death-penalty system so reliable that innocents on death row can be made a thing of the past." This belief is at the core of the Justice for All Act, passed in October 2004; the law provides funding for states to pay for postconviction testing and mandates that biological evidence in federal cases must be preserved.

When handled properly, DNA evidence is more reliable than any other form of evidence. It can definitively establish that an accused person was at the location of a crime. As writer Franklin E. Zimring explains, "Careful DNA matches with good samples will either implicate the subject of the match or exclude him; there are very few equivocal findings." However, the reliability of DNA testing depends on careful police and lab work in the collection, storage, and processing of DNA evidence. Untrained personnel, careless collection procedures, or deliberate tampering can lead to unreliable, misleading, or inaccurate results. In 2005 problems emerged in a number of leading crime labs, including those in Virginia, Oklahoma, and the national FBI laboratory, leading to a reexamination of cases based on evidence coming from these labs. As attorney Peter Neufeld said in a May 2, 2005, *Washington Post* article, "DNA is the most reliable and the most regulated of all the forensic sciences. But every time you have human beings involved, mistakes can occur."

DNA technology also promises to increase fairness in the application of the death penalty. Using such technology means that scientific testing standards will apply to all defendants equally. Moreover, DNA testing is free from color, class, ethnic, age, or gender bias. DNA testing allows justice to be blind to such differences in the accused. At the same time, DNA testing also exacerbates problems with fairness. Where a defendant lives can make a difference as to whether he or she will have the benefit of DNA technology because some states have not yet set up DNA labs. In other states the backlog at labs is so great that a test might take years to complete. Moreover, if defendants' attorneys fail to request DNA testing at the right time in the trial, the defendants may not have access to a technology that could conceivably clear them. Finally, DNA evidence is only available in about 25 percent of death penalty cases. According to the Death Penalty Information Center, of the 119 prisoners who have been exonerated, only 14 exonerations have been based on DNA testing.

The potential for increased justice and fairness also affects public confidence in the death penalty. According to a May 2005 Gallup poll, public confidence that the system only executes the guilty has grown with the increased use of DNA testing. As writer Robert Pambianco asserts, "If DNA evidence . . . can be used to remove any remaining doubt about a prisoner's guilt . . . far from undermining confidence in capital punishment, DNA evidence will only help increase the certainty about the guilt of those sentenced to die." Likewise, juries are able to draw on the evidence provided by scientific experts to render their decisions more confidently.

Paradoxically, however, DNA technology also reveals the system's flaws. As Zimring points out, "DNA undermines the myth of 'infallibility'. When DNA evidence contradicts eyewitness testimony in a case where biological samples were available, it weakens the trust that can be placed in eyewitness testimony even where biological evidence is not available." Moreover, as some experts point out, juries and the public might place too much confidence on expert testimony and DNA evidence without considering the ways such evidence can be manipulated.

Thus, while DNA evidence is an important tool in protecting the innocent and punishing the guilty, it cannot end the death penalty debate. As Daniel Avila, the Massachusetts Catholic Conference associate director for policy and research, reminds the public, "Even if one were able to determine with 100 percent confidence that a particular person were guilty of a particular offense, the question would remain whether the death of that person is absolutely necessary for the safety of society."

The issues raised by the use of DNA testing in death penalty trials promise to be at the center of the death penalty debate for years to come. The four chapters of *Opposing Viewpoints: The Death Penalty* explore contemporary views on these questions: Is the Death Penalty Just? Does the Death Penalty Deter Crime? Is the Death Penalty Applied Fairly? Should the Death Penalty Be Reformed? In this anthology authors debate the essential issues surrounding the use of the death penalty in the United States.

CHAPTER 1

Is the Death Penalty Just?

Chapter Preface

Any discussion of the death penalty in the United States inevitably must include mention of the concept of justice, a term complicated by its two connotations. In the first place, justice means the administration of the law. When the question "Is the death penalty just?" is raised, it is important to consider the legality of the death penalty. In the second place, justice also connotes both fair and reasonable treatment. In this context it is important to consider the moral rightness of the death penalty. Thus, when legal scholars, journalists, and the American public debate the death penalty, they raise two vital, yet sometimes contradictory questions: "Is the death penalty legal under the Constitution of the United States?" And, "Is the death penalty morally acceptable?"

Those who support the death penalty argue that the Constitution allows each state to decide for itself whether or not to impose the death penalty within certain federal guidelines. These analysts believe that the death penalty is legal. In addition, people who support the death penalty believe that it is the only just response to an egregious murder. In the U.S. Supreme Court case *Gregg v. Georgia* the Court observed, "The decision that capital punishment may be the appropriate sanction in extreme cases is an expression of the community's belief that certain crimes are themselves so grievous an affront to humanity that the only adequate response may be the penalty of death." Only execution, proponents believe, provides retribution for heinous crimes against victims and society. Death penalty proponents, in order to maintain public safety by permanently removing offenders from society, are willing to risk the execution of innocent people because of error. Paul Cassell points out in *Debating the Death Penalty* that there has not been "a credible case of an innocent person who has been actually executed in recent years." He continues, "Clearly . . . the innocent are far more at risk from allowing . . . dangerous convicts to live than from executing them."

On the other hand, those who would like to abolish the death penalty argue that the death penalty violates the Constitution, particularly the eighth amendment, which prohibits cruel and unusual punishment. The American Civil

Liberties Union, for example, notes that "the history of capital punishment is replete with examples of botched executions. But no execution is painless, whether botched or not, and all executions are certainly cruel." In addition, it contends that the death penalty is morally suspect, and that the danger of executing an innocent person far outweighs any benefit that might be had from the execution of a guilty person. Moreover, it asserts that there are classes of individuals, such as the mentally incapacitated and juveniles, who must be exempt from execution.

In 2005 the U.S. Supreme Court confronted these issues in considering the juvenile death penalty. In a narrowly decided opinion, the Court ruled that executing juveniles is no longer legal, nor is it morally right. While this decision is now the law of the land, it has not stopped debate about whether or not the death penalty is just. The writers of the viewpoints in this chapter analyze justice from both legal and moral perspectives.

> *"For me . . . the constitutionality of the death penalty is not a difficult, soul-wrenching question. It was clearly permitted when the Eighth Amendment was adopted. . . . And so it is clearly permitted today."*

The Death Penalty Is Just

Antonin Scalia

In the following viewpoint Antonin Scalia argues that the death penalty is just on both legal and religious grounds. It is legally just because it is permitted by the U.S. Constitution. It is religiously just because governments (not individuals) are given moral authority by God to uphold laws and to impose just retribution on wrongdoers. Scalia finds the death penalty a punishment appropriate and just for heinous crimes. Scalia is a U.S. Supreme Court justice.

As you read, consider the following questions:

1. What does Scalia mean when he says that "the Constitution . . . is not living but dead—or, as I prefer to put it, enduring"?
2. What, according to Scalia, is the only choice for judges who believe that the death penalty is immoral?
3. What are two reasons Scalia gives for thinking that the death penalty might be "more, rather than less necessary" in contemporary society?

Antonin Scalia, "God's Justice and Ours," *First Things: The Journal of Religion, Culture and Public Life*, May 2002, pp. 17–21. Copyright © 2002 by First Things 123. Reproduced by permission.

B efore proceeding to discuss the morality of capital punishment, I want to make clear that my views on the subject have nothing to do with how I vote in capital cases that come before the Supreme Court. That statement would not be true if I subscribed to the conventional fallacy that the Constitution is a "living document"—that is, a text that means from age to age whatever the society (or perhaps the Court) thinks it ought to mean. . . .

If I subscribed to the proposition that I am authorized (indeed, I suppose compelled) to intuit and impose our "maturing" society's "evolving standards of decency," this essay would be a preview of my next vote in a death penalty case. As it is, however, the Constitution that I interpret and apply is not living but dead—or, as I prefer to put it, enduring. It means today not what current society (much less the Court) thinks it ought to mean, but what it meant when it was adopted. For me, therefore, the constitutionality of the death penalty is not a difficult, soul-wrenching question. It was clearly permitted when the Eighth Amendment was adopted (not merely for murder, by the way, but for all felonies—including, for example, horse-thieving, as anyone can verify by watching a western movie). And so it is clearly permitted today. There is plenty of room within this system for "evolving standards of decency," but the instrument of evolution (or, if you are more tolerant of the Court's approach, the herald that evolution has occurred) is not the nine lawyers who sit on the Supreme Court of the United States, but the Congress of the United States and the legislatures of the fifty states, who may, within their own jurisdictions, restrict or abolish the death penalty as they wish.

But while my views on the morality of the death penalty have nothing to do with how I vote as a judge, they have a lot to do with whether I can or should be a judge at all. To put the point in the blunt terms employed by Justice Harold Blackmun towards the end of his career on the bench, when he announced that he would henceforth vote (as Justices William Brennan and Thurgood Marshall had previously done) to overturn all death sentences, when I sit on a Court that reviews and affirms capital convictions, I am part of "the machinery of death." My vote, when joined with at least four others, is, in most cases, the last step that permits an execution to proceed. I could not take part in that process if I believed what was being done to be immoral. . . .

Judges as Agents of Death

With the death penalty . . . I am part of the criminal-law machinery that imposes death—which extends from the indictment, to the jury conviction, to rejection of the last appeal. I am aware of the ethical principle that one can give "material cooperation" to the immoral act of another when the evil that would attend failure to cooperate is even greater (for example, helping a burglar tie up a householder where the alternative is that the burglar would kill the householder). I doubt whether that doctrine is even applicable to the trial judges and jurors who must themselves determine that the death sentence will be imposed. It seems to me these individuals are not merely engaged in "material cooperation" with someone else's action, but are themselves decreeing death on behalf of the state.

The same is true of appellate judges in those states where they are charged with "reweighing" the mitigating and aggravating factors and determining de novo [over again] whether the death penalty should be imposed: they are themselves decreeing death. Where (as is the case in the federal system) the appellate judge merely determines that the sentence pronounced by the trial court is in accordance with law, perhaps the principle of material cooperation could be applied. But as I have said, that principle demands that the good deriving from the cooperation exceed the evil which is assisted. I find it hard to see how any appellate judge could find this condition to be met, unless he believes retaining his seat on the bench (rather than resigning) is somehow essential to preservation of the society—which is of course absurd. . . .

I pause here to emphasize the point that in my view the choice for the judge who believes the death penalty to be immoral is resignation, rather than simply ignoring duly enacted, constitutional laws and sabotaging death penalty cases. He has, after all, taken an oath to apply the laws and has been given no power to supplant them with rules of his own. Of course if he feels strongly enough he can go beyond mere resignation and lead a political campaign to abolish the death penalty—and if that fails, lead a revolution. But rewrite the laws he cannot do. . . .

It is a matter of great consequence to me, therefore, whether the death penalty is morally acceptable. As a Roman Catholic—and being unable to jump out of my skin—I cannot discuss that issue without reference to Christian tradition and the Church's Magisterium [official teaching of the Catholic Church].

The Morality of the Death Penalty

The death penalty is undoubtedly wrong unless one accords to the state a scope of moral action that goes beyond what is permitted to the individual. In my view, the major impetus behind modern aversion to the death penalty is the equation of private morality with governmental morality. This is a predictable (though I believe erroneous and regrettable) reaction to modern, democratic self-government.

Few doubted the morality of the death penalty in the age that believed in the divine right of kings. Or even in earlier times. St. Paul had this to say (I am quoting, as you might expect, the King James version):

> Let every soul be subject unto the higher powers. For there is no power but of God: the powers that be are ordained of God. Whosoever therefore resisteth the power, resisteth the ordinance of God: and they that resist shall receive to themselves damnation. For rulers are not a terror to good works, but to the evil. Wilt thou then not be afraid of the power? Do that which is good, and thou shalt have praise of the same: for he is the minister of God to thee for good. But if thou do that which is evil, be afraid; for he beareth not the sword in vain: for he is the minister of God, a revenger to execute wrath upon him that doeth evil. Wherefore ye must needs be subject, not only for wrath, but also for conscience sake. (Romans 13:1–5)

This is not the Old Testament, I emphasize, but St. Paul. One can understand his words as referring only to lawfully constituted authority, or even only to lawfully constituted authority that rules justly. But the *core* of his message is that government—however you want to limit that concept—derives its moral authority from God. It is the "minister of

God" with powers to "revenge," to "execute wrath," including even wrath by the sword (which is unmistakably a reference to the death penalty). Paul of course did not believe that the *individual* possessed any such powers. Only a few lines before this passage, he wrote, "Dearly beloved, avenge not yourselves, but rather give place unto wrath: for it is written, Vengeance is mine; I will repay, saith the Lord." And in this world the Lord repaid—did justice—through His minister, the state.

Locher. © 1994 by the *Chicago Tribune*. Reproduced by permission of Knight Ridder/Tribune Information.

These passages from Romans represent the consensus of Western thought until very recent times. Not just of Christian or religious thought, but of secular thought regarding the powers of the state. That consensus has been upset, I think, by the emergence of democracy. It is easy to see the hand of the Almighty behind rulers whose forebears, in the dim mists of history, were supposedly anointed by God, or who at least obtained their thrones in awful and unpredictable battles whose outcome was determined by the Lord of Hosts, that is, the Lord of Armies. It is much more difficult to see the hand of God—or any higher moral authority —behind the fools and rogues (as the losers would have it) whom we ourselves elect to do our own will. How can their power to avenge—to vindicate the "public order"—be any greater than our own?

So it is no accident, I think, that the modern view that the death penalty is immoral is centered in the West. That has little to do with the fact that the West has a Christian tradition, and everything to do with the fact that the West is the home of democracy. Indeed, it seems to me that the more Christian a country is the *less* likely it is to regard the death penalty as immoral. Abolition has taken its firmest hold in post-Christian Europe, and has least support in the church-going United States. I attribute that to the fact that, for the believing Christian, death is no big deal. Intentionally killing an innocent person is a big deal: it is a grave sin, which causes one to lose his soul. But losing this life, in exchange for the next? The Christian attitude is reflected in the words Robert Bolt's play has Thomas More saying to the headsman: "Friend, be not afraid of your office. You send me to God." And when Cranmer asks whether he is sure of that, More replies, "He will not refuse one who is so blithe to go to Him." For the nonbeliever, on the other hand, to deprive a man of his life is to end his existence. What a horrible act!

Besides being *less* likely to regard death as an utterly cataclysmic punishment, the Christian is also *more* likely to regard punishment in general as deserved. The doctrine of free will—the ability of man to resist temptations to evil, which God will not permit beyond man's capacity to resist—is central to the Christian doctrine of salvation and damnation, heaven and hell. The post-Freudian secularist, on the other hand, is more inclined to think that people are what their history and circumstances have made them, and there is little sense in assigning blame.

The Moral Authority of the Government

Of course those who deny the authority of a government to exact vengeance are not entirely logical. Many crimes—for example, domestic murder in the heat of passion—are neither deterred by punishment meted out to others nor likely to be committed a second time by the same offender. Yet opponents of capital punishment do not object to sending such an offender to prison, perhaps for life. Because he *deserves* punishment. Because it is *just*.

Justice Demands the Death Penalty

We who support capital punishment for murder—and only for murder—ask opponents to acknowledge that allowing all murderers to keep their lives after deliberately taking others' lives is, at the very least, unjust.

If a man steals your bicycle and society allows him to keep and ride around on that bicycle, most of us would find that profoundly unjust. Why, then, is it just to allow everyone who steals a life to keep his own?

The answer is that it is not just. Indeed, it is a cosmic injustice.

Dennis Prager, *Milwaukee Journal Sentinel: JS Online*, June 9, 2001. www. jsonline.com.

The mistaken tendency to believe that a democratic government, being nothing more than the composite will of its individual citizens, has no more moral power or authority than they do as individuals has adverse effects in other areas as well. It fosters civil disobedience, for example, which proceeds on the assumption that what the individual citizen considers an unjust law—even if it does not compel *him* to act unjustly—need not be obeyed. St. Paul would not agree. "Ye must needs be subject," he said, "not only for wrath, but also for conscience sake." For conscience sake. The reaction of people of faith to this tendency of democracy to obscure the divine authority behind government should not be resignation to it, but the resolution to combat it as effectively as possible. We have done that in this country (and continental Europe has not) by preserving in our public life many visible reminders that—in the words of a Supreme Court opinion from the 1940s—"we are a religious people, whose institutions presuppose a Supreme Being." These reminders include: "In God we trust" on our coins, "one nation, under God" in our Pledge of Allegiance, the opening of sessions of our legislatures with a prayer, the opening of sessions of my Court with "God save the United States and this Honorable Court," annual Thanksgiving proclamations issued by our President at the direction of Congress, and constant invocations of divine support in the speeches of our political leaders, which often conclude, "God bless America." All this, as I say, is most un-European, and helps explain why our people are more inclined to understand, as St. Paul did, that government carries the sword as "the minister of God," to "execute wrath" upon the evildoer. . . .

It will come as no surprise from what I have said that I do not agree with the encyclical *Evangelium Vitae* [letter to Roman Catholic bishops from the pope] and the new Catholic catechism (or the very latest version of the new Catholic catechism), according to which the death penalty can only be imposed to protect rather than avenge, and that since it is (in most modern societies) not necessary for the former purpose, it is wrong: . . . [Here is] the following passage from the encyclical:

> It is clear that, for these [permissible purposes of penal justice] to be achieved, the nature and extent of the punishment must be carefully evaluated and decided upon, and ought not go to the extreme of executing the offender except in cases of absolute necessity: *in other words, when it would not be possible otherwise to defend society. Today, however, as a result of steady improvements in the organization of the penal system, such cases are very rare, if not practically nonexistent.* (Emphases deleted and added.) . . .

How in the world can modernity's "steady improvements in the organization of the penal system" render the death penalty less condign [appropriate] for a particularly heinous crime? One might think that commitment to a really horrible penal system . . . might be almost as bad as death. But nice clean cells with television sets, exercise rooms, meals designed by nutritionists, and conjugal visits? That would seem to render the death penalty more, rather than less, necessary. So also would the greatly increased capacity for evil—the greatly increased power to produce moral "disorder"—placed in individual hands by modern technology. Could St. Paul or St. Thomas even have envisioned a crime by an individual (as opposed to one by a ruler, such as Herod's slaughter of the innocents) as enormous as that of [Oklahoma City bomber] Timothy McVeigh or of the men who destroyed three thousand innocents in the World Trade Center [on September 11, 2001]? If just retribution is a legitimate purpose (indeed, the principal legitimate purpose) of capital punishment, can one possibly say with a straight face that nowadays death would "rarely if ever" be appropriate?

So I take the encyclical and the latest, hot-off-the-presses version of the catechism (a supposed encapsulation of the "deposit" of faith and the Church's teaching regarding a moral order that does not change) to mean that retribution is not a valid purpose of capital punishment. Unlike such other hard Catholic doctrines as the prohibition of birth control and of abortion, this is not a moral position that the Church has always—or indeed *ever before*—maintained. There have been Christian opponents of the death penalty, just as there have been Christian pacifists, but neither of those positions has ever been that of the Church. The current predominance of opposition to the death penalty is the legacy of Napoleon, Hegel, and Freud rather than St. Paul and St. Augustine. I mentioned earlier Thomas More, who has long been regarded in this country as the patron saint of lawyers, and who has recently been declared by the Vatican the patron saint of politicians (I am not sure that is a promotion). One of the charges leveled by that canonized saint's detractors was that, as Lord Chancellor, he was too quick to impose the death penalty.

I am therefore happy to learn from the canonical experts I have consulted that the position set forth in *Evangelium Vitae* and in the latest version of the Catholic catechism does not purport to be binding teaching—that is, it need not be accepted by practicing Catholics, though they must give it thoughtful and respectful consideration. It would be remarkable to think otherwise—that a couple of paragraphs in an encyclical almost entirely devoted not to crime and punishment but to abortion and euthanasia was intended authoritatively to sweep aside (if one could) two thousand years of Christian teaching.

So I have given this new position thoughtful and careful consideration—and I disagree. That is not to say I favor the death penalty (I am judicially and judiciously neutral on that point); it is only to say that I do not find the death penalty immoral.

"The death penalty erodes all three commitments—to equality, to justice, and to the rule of law."

The Death Penalty Is Unjust

Anthony G. Amsterdam

In the following viewpoint Anthony G. Amsterdam asserts that the principle of equal justice under the law is corrupted by the unjust application of the death penalty. According to the author, prosecutors make arbitrary decisions that ultimately lead to the death penalty for some defendants and life terms for others. In addition, says the author, studies show that more blacks than whites are sentenced to death, proving that capital punishment is applied unevenly. Finally, he maintains that the legal system bends the law in order to sentence offenders to death. For example, jurors in capital cases must be willing to vote for a death sentence or they are disqualified, leading to juries that are more prone to impose the death penalty. Amsterdam is a professor at the New York University School of Law.

As you read, consider the following questions:
1. What are some of the decisions that prosecutors make that affect death penalty sentencing, according to Amsterdam?
2. What effect does the race of the murder victim have on death penalty sentencing in studies cited by Amsterdam?
3. What was the primary question in *Ring v. Arizona*?

Anthony G. Amsterdam, "Courtroom Contortions," *The American Prospect*, vol. 15, July 1, 2004, pp. A19–21. Copyright © 2004 by The American Prospect, Inc., 11 Beacon Street, Suite 1120, Boston, MA 02108. All rights reserved. Reproduced with permission.

O ne cost this country pays for the death penalty is that its courts are constantly compelled to corrupt the law in order to uphold death sentences. That corruption soils the character of the United States as a nation dedicated to equal justice under law.

This is not the only price we pay for being one of the very few democracies in the world that retains capital punishment in the 21st century. But it is a significant item on the cost side of the cost-benefit ledger, something that each thinking person ought to balance in deciding whether he or she supports capital punishment. And it warrants discussion because this cost is little understood. I have spent much of my time for the past 40 years representing death-sentenced inmates in appeals at every level of the state and federal judicial systems, and I am only lately coming to realize how large a tax the death penalty imposes on the quality of justice in those systems.

The western face of the U.S. Supreme Court building bears the motto "Equal Justice Under Law." Court opinions frequently quote this motto to summarize the basic commitments of our constitutional democracy. The death penalty erodes all three commitments—to equality, to justice, and to the rule of law.

Erratic and Haphazard Decisions

In the first place, death sentences are handed out in a way that belies our pretensions of evenhandedness, fairness, and legal regularity. Whether a person convicted of murder will end up sentenced to death or to prison depends upon a series of discretionary decisions by the prosecutor in each case—what crime to charge, whether to engage in plea bargaining (and on what terms), whether to seek a death sentence—and another discretionary decision by the sentencing judge or jury.

These decisions are individually erratic and collectively haphazard, producing one or two death sentences and a dozen or two dozen lesser sentences out of every group of cases that is factually, legally, and rationally indistinguishable as regards the nature and circumstances of the crime and the character and record of the defendant. For example, there are currently 72 young people in 12 states awaiting execution for murders committed when they were under 18 years old. Yet a Virginia jury sentenced Lee Boyd Malvo, one of the Washington-area snipers, to life, not death, and the overwhelming majority of juveniles who—like the 72 now on death row—have committed crimes less egregious than Malvo's are not sentenced to die.

Next, as legal appeals proceed, a mirror-image kind of inequality develops. For every condemned defendant whose death sentence is set aside by a reviewing court on the ground of some trial error or constitutional violation, there are a dozen or more defendants who do *not* get their death sentences set aside despite indistinguishable trial errors or constitutional violations in their cases. Courts supposedly applying general legal rules turn out decisions that are almost as unpredictable and inexplicable as the decisions of prosecutors and sentencing juries making ad hoc, case-specific judgments.

For example, in 2000 and 2003, the U.S. Supreme Court vacated the death sentences of Terry Williams in Virginia and Kevin Wiggins in Maryland after finding that the lawyers for these men had performed so incompetently at their sentencing trials that Williams and Wiggins were denied the "assistance of counsel" required by the Sixth Amendment. There is no doubt that the lawyers' performances were abysmal in both of these cases. But every practiced capital-defense attorney or prosecutor I know was amazed by the Court's *Williams* and *Wiggins* decisions, because all of us have seen case after case in which defendants received *worse* representation than these two men did and yet had their Sixth Amendment claims rejected by the lower courts and their requests for review summarily denied by the Supreme Court.

Racial Discrimination in Death Penalty Cases

Death sentences are meted out not only erratically but also discriminatorily, on the basis of race. Exhaustive studies done in connection with the *McCleskey v. Kemp* case that other lawyers and I took to the Supreme Court in 1986 demonstrated this deeply troubling pattern. In Georgia murder prosecutions between 1973 and 1979, 22 percent of black defendants who killed white victims were sentenced to death; 8 percent of white defendants who killed white victims were sentenced to death; 1 percent of black defendants who killed black victims were sentenced to death; and 3 percent of white defendants who killed black victims were sentenced to death. (Only 64 of the 2,500 homicide cases studied involved killings of blacks by whites, so the 3-percent figure represents two death sentences over a six-year period. The reason why bias against black defendants was not even more apparent was that most black defendants convicted of murder have killed black victims; almost no convictions are found of white defendants who have killed black victims; and virtually no defendant convicted of killing a black victim gets the death penalty.)

No factor other than race explained these patterns. The studies analyzed hundreds of factors relating to the crime, to the victim, and to the defendant in each case. The analysis with the greatest explanatory power showed that after controlling for nonracial factors, murderers of white victims received a death sentence 4.3 times more frequently than murderers of black victims. The race of the victim was as good a predictor of a capital sentence as the aggravating factors spelled out for jury consideration in the Georgia statute, like whether the defendant had a prior murder conviction or was the primary actor in the present murder. (Only 5 percent of Georgia killings resulted in a death sentence, yet, when more than 230 nonracial variables were controlled for, the death-sentencing rate was 6 percent higher in white-victim cases than in black-victim cases. In other words, a murderer incurred less risk of death by committing the murder in the first place than by selecting a white victim instead of a black one.) Newer studies in other states have consistently shown the same racially discriminatory pattern of capital sentencing.

More appalling than these statistics was the Supreme Court's reaction to them. In an opinion by Justice Lewis Powell Jr., a 5-to-4 majority conceded that the data before the Court "indicated a risk that racial considerations enter into capital sentencing determinations," but held that the courts have no constitutional power to remedy this situation. Justice Powell's *McCleskey* opinion offered a series of elaborate reasons for its conclusions, but the bottom line was that if the courts undertook to review claims of race discrimination in capital sentencing, they would also be obliged to review claims of discrimination by other subgroups disfavored in the capital-sentencing lottery, and the death penalty would be rendered unenforceable as a practical matter.

Four years later, after his retirement from the Court, Powell told his biographer that he'd changed his mind and would have changed his vote in *McCleskey* if he could. He had become convinced that capital punishment cannot be administered with the fairness and consistency necessary to satisfy the Constitution. Nevertheless, the Supreme Court has refused to reconsider its 1987 ruling.

Court Reversals Lead to Injustice

To be sure, the Court does sometimes reverse itself on death-penalty issues. But these "corrections" expose additional problems with the penalty. Consider the 2002 decision in *Ring v. Arizona*.

The question in *Ring* was whether a convicted defendant could be made eligible for a death sentence on the basis of facts found by a judge rather than a jury. The question arose because in Arizona (and six other states), after a jury convicted a defendant of first-degree murder, additional aggravating circumstances had to be found in order to support a death sentence, and these findings were made by the trial judge (or a three-judge panel), *not* by the jury. In 1990, this Arizona procedure had been upheld by the Supreme Court against the argument that it violated the right to jury trial guaranteed by the Constitution. But in 2000, the Court had held, in a hate-crime case, that the constitutional right to jury trial was violated by a procedure that allowed a defendant convicted of a noncapital crime to be sentenced to a longer term of imprisonment than the maximum prescribed for that crime if a judge, without a jury, found that the crime was aggravated by being racially motivated.

In the *Ring* case, lawyers for a condemned inmate argued that Arizona's capital-sentencing procedure involved the same constitutional defect that the Court had found in the 2000 hate-crime case. The Supreme Court agreed, overruled its dozen-year-old decision upholding the Arizona procedure, and declared the procedure unconstitutional.

The same arguments that were made to the Court and accepted by it in the 2002 *Ring* case and in the 2000 hate-crime case had been made to the Court and rejected by it in its 1990 Arizona decision and also in a 1984 Florida case challenging an analogous judge-sentencing procedure. Those arguments were based on what the Framers of the Constitution, in light of preceding centuries of English history, must have meant the constitutional right of jury trial to include. Nothing relevant or rational made those arguments any more convincing legally in 2000 or 2002 than in 1984 or 1990. The Supreme Court simply woke up to the arguments 10 years too late to save the 22 men who were put to death in Arizona between 1990 and 2002 under a procedure that the Court belatedly discovered was unconstitutional. And constitutional-law experts predict that, in a decision expected in the next few weeks, the Supreme Court will declare that the *Ring* decision is not "retroactive" and therefore does not invalidate the death sentences of 87 additional persons who are now on Arizona's death row under the sentencing procedure invalidated in *Ring*.[1] The 87 could then be put to death even after the *Ring* decision—though their death sentences were imposed by a process *Ring* held incompatible with the Constitution.

The Legality of the Death Penalty

All this may well cause you to question the evenhandedness and fairness of the death penalty as it is used in this country today. But what about its legality? Aren't the practices and consequences I've described strictly lawful, however dubious from the standpoints of equality and justice? That depends on whether you believe that it is legally proper for courts to twist the ordinary rules of law in order to uphold death sentences and authorize executions that the rules would not tolerate without twisting.

Remember the 1987 *McCleskey* case, in which the Supreme Court was faced with the question of whether courts should review claims of race discrimination in capital sentencing

1. The Supreme Court determined on June 24, 2004, that *Ring* was not retroactive.

based on solid statistical evidence. The Court held that they should not, although it admitted that its precedents required courts to hear claims of race discrimination in jury selection and in governmental- and private-employment practices, based on the same kind of statistical evidence. The Court's reason for this result came close to a frank admission that the administration of capital punishment would grind to a halt if courts took seriously the challenge of ensuring that death sentences are not the products of racial bias.

At Odds with America's Best Traditions

One thing is clear: no matter how hard we try, we cannot overcome the inevitable fallibility of being human. That fallibility means that we will not be able to apply the death penalty in a fair and just manner. . . .

The death penalty is at odds with our best traditions. It is wrong and it is immoral. The adage 'two wrongs do not make a right,' could not be more appropriate here. Our nation has long ago done away with other barbaric punishments like whipping and cutting off the ears of suspected criminals. Just as our nation did away with these punishments as contrary to our humanity and ideals, it is time to abolish the death penalty as we enter the next century. The continued viability of our justice system as a truly just system requires that we do so. . . .

Let us step away from the culture of violence and restore fairness and integrity to our criminal justice system. As we head into the next millennium, let us leave this archaic practice behind.

Russ Feingold, statement on the Federal Death Penalty Abolition Act, November 16, 2000. www.senate.gov.

Similarly, in a 1986 case, the Supreme Court was confronted with evidence that the universal practice of "death-qualifying" capital juries—that is, of excluding from jury service any juror who is conscientiously unable to consider voting for a death sentence—had the effect of making capital juries more prone to convict and less willing to give defendants the benefit of the doubt on the issue of guilt or innocence. The Court held that even if this was so, capital defendants are not entitled to have the issue of their guilt decided by a jury that is neutral and impartial according to the standard of the ordinary juries that try all other kinds of criminal cases. It reasoned that because the state is entitled to punish convicted murderers with death, it must be entitled to select juries that will impose a death sentence—and if the only way to get such juries is to compromise ordinary standards of impartiality, so be it. The Court rejected the suggestion that the state's interest in obtaining death sentences could be served by impaneling a death-qualified jury to determine sentence, *after* a conviction, either by forming a new jury or by substituting alternate jurors from the guilt-phase trial for any jurors who could not consider voting for death. The Court said that states employing the death penalty can reasonably conclude that such procedures are too burdensome or inefficient.

Equal Justice Under the Law?

The lesson of these Supreme Court decisions is unmistakable. If ordinary judicial scrutiny of apparent patterns of race discrimination cannot be conducted without hampering the states' efficient pursuit of death sentences, judicial scrutiny will be forsworn. If ordinary standards of fairness for criminal-trial juries cannot be maintained without hampering the states' efficient pursuit of death sentences, those standards will be forsworn and juries uncommonly prone to convict will be permitted to do so. When the ordinary fabric of constitutional law needs to be twisted to make the death penalty enforceable, the necessary twists will be made.

This lesson helps us understand the *Ring* case. Why did the Supreme Court suddenly discover in 2000 and 2002 a centuries-old right to jury trial that had escaped its notice in 1984 and 1990? Because in 1984 and 1990, that right was being claimed on behalf of death-sentenced inmates, and its recognition would have stopped their executions. In this context, the Court brushed aside the claim as unworthy of serious consideration. In 2000, the same claim was made on behalf of a convicted noncapital felon challenging an increase in the length of his prison sentence based on a judge-made finding that the crime was motivated by racial bigotry. Here the Court gave the claim serious consideration and upheld it. Then, in 2002, the logical impossibility of distinguishing a death sentence that depended solely upon judge-made findings of fact from a prison sentence that depended solely upon judge-made findings of fact shamed the Court into recognizing that its earlier decisions had been—quite literally—dead wrong.

So, were the 22 prisoners who were executed in Arizona alone under the Court's dead-wrong decision upholding the Arizona capital-sentencing scheme in 1990 lawfully put to death? Or the 87 prisoners whom the Court has held can still be executed after it admitted that its 1990 decision was wrong? Not, I believe, if you take lawful to mean what it surely pretends to mean as engraved on the Supreme Court's facade in the phrase "Equal Justice Under Law."

"While there are many reasons to turn off the machinery of death, perhaps the most compelling is the ever-present possibility of executing innocent people."

The Death Penalty Kills Innocent People

Daily Record Advisory Board

In this viewpoint the editorial advisory board of Baltimore's *Daily Record* argues that because all human institutions are flawed, it is inevitable that errors in death penalty sentencing will be made and innocent people will be killed. The board cites studies indicating that numerous innocent people have indeed been sentenced to death, and it urges the state of Maryland to join many other states and nations that have abolished the death penalty. The editorial advisory board is a group of journalists and legal experts who establish the editorial position of the *Daily Record* on important controversial issues.

As you read, consider the following questions:

1. Who is Kirk Bloodsworth and how did he escape execution?
2. Who is Cameron Todd Willingham and why was he executed?
3. What are some of the organizations the editorial advisory board cites as being opposed to the death penalty?

Daily Record Advisory Board, "It Is Time to Say 'Enough' to Death Penalty," *Daily Record*, December 20, 2004. Copyright © 2004 by Dolan Media Newswires. Reproduced by permission.

W e have, in Maryland, a state government program that has an unacceptable error rate, is applied unfairly, is ineffective and extremely costly, and is considered atavistic by almost every western democracy and the majority of other countries across the globe. Here in the U.S., 12 states have recognized that the program is fatally flawed and cannot be fixed. It has been abolished in Alaska, Hawaii, Iowa, Maine, Massachusetts, Michigan, Minnesota, North Dakota, Rhode Island, Vermont, West Virginia and Wisconsin. It is time for Maryland to join their ranks as the thirteenth state.

The program we are referring to is state-sponsored execution. In addition to the 12 states that have abolished the death penalty, there are six states that still have death statutes on their books, but have not performed an execution since 1976. They are Connecticut, Kansas, New Hampshire, New Jersey, New York and South Dakota.

Supreme Court Justice Harry A. Blackmun eloquently captured our opinion in his dissent from the Supreme Court's decision to deny review in a Texas death penalty case, *Callins v. Collins*, 510 U.S. 1141, 1143 (1994):

> Twenty years have passed since this court declared that the death penalty must be imposed fairly and with reasonable consistency or not at all, and despite the effort of the states and courts to devise legal formulas and procedural rules to meet this . . . challenge, the death penalty remains fraught with arbitrariness, discrimination . . . and mistake. . . . From this day forward, I no longer shall tinker with the machinery of death . . . I feel . . . obligated simply to concede that the death penalty experiment has failed. It is virtually self-evident to me now that no combination of procedural rules or substantive regulations ever can save the death penalty from its inherent constitutional deficiencies.

Innocence and Error

While there are many reasons to turn off the machinery of death, perhaps the most compelling is the ever-present possibility of executing innocent people. Some of us would support the death penalty if the criminal justice system could guarantee that no innocent people would ever be executed. We recognize, however, that this is not a perfect world, we are not perfect beings, and our criminal justice system, while necessary, is inalterably flawed. To address this, many opportunities for reconsideration are built into the system. But they too are flawed, and there is no reconsideration that will raise the dead.

Since 1973, 117 people serving time on death rows across the country have been exonerated and freed from prisons. The major reasons for their wrongful capital convictions have included mistaken identifications, inaccurate laboratory evidence, police misconduct, prosecutorial misconduct, bad lawyering, false confessions, and false witness testimony (especially the testimony of informants and fellow inmates). Can we say with confidence that there are no other inmates on death rows, beyond these 117, who have been wrongfully convicted? Do we know, with certainty, that there will be no future wrongful capital conviction? No one, being honest, can answer "yes" to these questions. That we ("we" operating collectively as the state) may have killed, and may yet kill, an innocent person, is an uncertainty, and a horror, that is intolerable.

We can be certain that we have had, at least, one innocent person on our death row in Maryland. Kirk Bloodsworth was sentenced to death for the 1984 rape and murder of nine-year-old Dawn Hamilton in Baltimore County. In 1987, after serving two years on death row, his sentence was overturned. Baltimore County prosecuted and convicted him again, and this time he was sentenced to life in prison without the possibility of parole. In 1993, he became the first of 13 inmates who had served time on death row to be exonerated by post-conviction DNA testing. After spending nearly nine years behind bars, the former marine and Eastern Shore waterman was exonerated, pardoned and released.

Bloodsworth is free because he had a stroke of good fortune. Barry Scheck's Innocence Project at Cardozo University tested his DNA. Unfortunately, DNA evidence is only available in a fraction of all first-degree murder cases.

A cloud of suspicion still hovered over Bloodsworth until the real killer was found almost 10 years later. Kimberley Shay Ruffner's DNA came up as a match to DNA found at the scene of Dawn's murder, and he confessed to committing the crime alone. In contrast to the death sentence received at Bloodsworth's first trial, Ruffner received life imprisonment for having committed the same murder, rape and sexual assault.

Recently, the *Chicago Tribune* reported that Cameron Todd Willingham, who was executed in Texas in February, had been convicted based on forensic evidence that has now been discredited. Willingham, who declared his innocence with his last words, was convicted of arson and murder for a fire that burnt down his house with his three young daughters trapped inside. Gerald Hurst, a prominent chemist who has investigated many fires, examined the evidence and said, "There's nothing to suggest to any reasonable arson investigator that this was an arson fire." At the request of the *Tribune*, three other fire investigators examined the evidence, and agreed with Hurst.

In 1990, Jesse Tafero was executed in Florida. He and his wife, Sonia Jacobs, had received the death penalty for the murder of a state trooper. Two years after Jesse's execution, a federal court vacated Sonia's sentence and released her, because her conviction (as was Jesse's) was based on the perjured testimony of an ex-convict who turned state's witness to avoid a death sentence. Had Jesse still been alive in 1992, he would surely have been released with his wife—but death is an irreversible penalty.

In Illinois, Gov. Ryan, staggered by a series of wrongful capital convictions, recently declared a moratorium on executions. He pardoned four death row inmates and commuted the sentences of 167 others.

In addition to innocence or execution, inmates are also removed from Maryland's death row due to trial errors. Kevin Williams, John Miller, Kenneth Collins and others had their death sentences reduced to lesser sentences because persistent lawyers uncovered prosecutorial or other errors at trial. As with innocence, it is impossible to be certain that all erroneous death penalty convictions have been or will be detected and corrected. We believe that no human being should be executed in a circumstance where having a good lawyer would have prevented the execution.

A Columbia University study of 5,760 capital cases across the country, between 1973 and 1995, found capital sentences persistently and systematically fraught with error that seriously undermines their reliability. Courts that reviewed these capital cases during the 23-year study, found serious reversible error in 68 percent of the cases. Fewer than 5 percent of all of the death sentences imposed over the 23-year period resulted in executions. The cumbersome and expensive machinery of death wastes enormous resources for a very small, and perhaps fatally wrong, outcome.

Bias and Inequity

Claims that the death penalty is imposed in a biased manner are being brought before the courts. Maryland death row inmate Heath Burch had been scheduled for execution the week of Dec. 6 [2004]. Prior to that date, a Prince Georges County judge granted a stay of execution so that Burch's attorneys can mount a legal challenge, which will include evidence of bias in the imposition of death sentences in Maryland. Prince George's County State's Attorney Glenn Ivey has agreed that the defense should have the opportunity to raise this evidence. If executed, Burch would be the first Prince George's County man to be executed since Lott Glover was hanged more than 50 years ago.[1]

Heath Burch is the first African-American inmate to have been scheduled for execution since the University of Maryland, College Park released its two-and-a-half-year comprehensive death penalty research study in 2003. His lawyers will use the study as part of their case, as will several other Maryland death row inmates.

The study, often referred to as the "Paternoster Study" after professor Raymond Paternoster, examined 1,300 death eligible murder cases in Maryland. The study controlled for differences in case characteristics, and revealed three variables in imposing death sentences that had statistically significant patterns of bias: the race of the victim (no bias was found based on the race of the offender), the combined races of offender and victim, and the location of the murder.

The study found that, even though 80 percent of the homicide victims in Maryland are African American, the

---

1. As of December 2005, Burch remained on death row.

death sentence is twice as likely to be imposed if the victim is white. In combination, African-American offenders who kill white victims are two and one-half times more likely to be sentenced to death than whites who kill whites. The study also found significant differences based on geography.

While some contend that it is acceptable for different counties to impose the death penalty to different degrees, we disagree. The death penalty statute is a state law that may vary state to state, but a law of this magnitude should be applied uniformly within a state. Marylanders are crossing jurisdictional boundaries constantly. It should not be the basis for life or death differences.

Increasing Number of Exonerations

Eight-Year Periods (through 8/04)

Richard C. Dieter, *Innocence and the Crisis in the American Death Penalty.* Death Penalty Information Center, September 2004. www.deathpenalty info.org.

The study notes that approximately 45 percent of all of the death sentences in Maryland are imposed in Baltimore County, even though Baltimore County has only 12 percent of Maryland's death-eligible murder cases. It also indicates that this phenomenon is not a result of the State's Attorney consistently seeking the death penalty in every death eligible Baltimore County case; rather, the study states that Baltimore County seeks the death penalty in only 65 percent of its death eligible cases.

The Supreme Court is also considering bias and the death penalty. On Dec. 6, the Court heard arguments in a case alleging that an almost all-white jury was unfairly biased against a black defendant. The defense displayed a manual used from 1960 to 1980 to train Dallas County prosecutors, which advises them to remove blacks and Jews from death penalty juries because they would be more sympathetic to criminal defendants. Earlier this year [2004], in a departure from previous opinions, the Supreme Court issued "stinging reversals" to three Texas death penalty cases on various grounds.

We believe that the vast majority of those who support the death penalty want to see it imposed in an unbiased manner and for the most heinous crimes, but this is not what happens. The system's inequity is harshly illustrated in the case of a Maryland man who was executed in 1997. Flint Gregory Hunt, high on drugs in a stolen car joyride gone wrong, killed Police Officer Vincent Adolfo. It was an unplanned heinous crime, and Hunt received the death penalty. Hunt's death by lethal injection was the first non-consensual execution in Maryland (John Thanos abandoned his appeals) in 36 years.

This stands in stark contrast to what happened to the murderer of Hunt's common-law wife, who was also brutally raped by her assailant. Although rape, like the killing of a police officer, is a statutory aggravating factor that shifts the balance toward a death sentence, Hunt's wife's rapist and killer was only sentenced to 30 years in prison for his planned heinous crimes. Hunt's son and other family members are left to grapple with this grim inequity.

Death penalty proponents may say that these biases should be cured by putting all murderers to death—an eye for an eye—rather than by abolishing the death penalty. This argument is logical, but quite futile. Our legal system and our human decency require us to attempt to weed the error out of death penalty cases. This is why the appeals process, nationally, takes an average of 11 years in capital cases.

Even if our legal system could handle the weight of protracted appeals in every murder case, Maryland would have to become a killing ground to keep up with the number of people being executed. We would have to grow the machinery of death into a massive and exorbitantly costly killing business to execute someone for every murder committed in the state. There would be executions every day. It will never happen, nor should it.

No Deterrence and High Costs

We should abolish the death penalty because, in addition to being flawed, biased and riddled with error, it does not deter other homicides and it costs us a great deal of money. The vast majority of studies across the country have concluded that the death penalty is not a deterrent that prevents other criminals from committing murder. The few that conclude otherwise, based on econometric analyses, have been harshly criticized for their methodology.

FBI statistics show that states with the death penalty have homicide rates that are 44 percent higher then those without it. According to the Bureau of Justice Statistics, the Southern U.S. has the highest murder rate, and accounts for 80 percent of all U.S. executions. The Northeast, which has less than 1 percent of all U.S. executions, has the lowest murder rate. The murder rate in the 12 states that have abolished the death penalty has remained consistently lower than the murder rate in states that still impose the death penalty.

Death penalty supporters may argue that the death penalty certainly is a deterrent for the individual who is executed. This is clearly true, but a sentence of life without the possibility of parole provides the same deterrent—and at a much lower cost.

While cost studies differ from state to state, they all find death penalty cases to be extremely expensive. States bear enormous costs to give inmates the opportunity to exhaust all of their appeal rights before being executed.

A 1993 comprehensive Duke University study found that the death penalty costs the state of North Carolina $2.16 million per execution over the cost of a non–death penalty murder case, including the cost of incarceration. According to the *Palm Beach Post*, enforcing the death penalty costs Florida $51 million a year above and beyond what it would cost if the state had to cover the expense of maintaining all first-degree murderers in prison with sentences of life without the possibility of parole.

As we go to press, Maryland has seven men on death row

(five are black; in all seven cases the victims were white, and four of the death-row inmates were prosecuted by Baltimore County).[2] While we don't know the exact cost per inmate, we think that the money spent on the necessary pre-execution legal process and on the executions, would have a far greater and more positive societal effect if it were spent on crime prevention.

Victims and Survivors

When considering the death penalty, we cannot avoid the issue of retribution for the victims' grieving families. We all have great sympathy for families that lose a loved one to the senseless act of murder, it is an unspeakable horror, leaving a gaping wound in the fabric of their lives. But retribution in the form of an execution may not be the best alternative for those families.

Judge Dana Levitz, a former Baltimore County prosecutor who still supports the death penalty, has cited "compassion" for the families as one of his reasons for not imposing the death penalty in certain cases. He recognizes that the long, drawn-out appeals process, which may result in remands and reduced sentences, may deny certain survivors the closure they need to move on following a tragic loss.

Even after years and years of appeals are exhausted, an execution may not bring real closure for the survivors. It is not uncommon, after an execution, to hear a family member say that the execution was "too quick," and that the murderer "didn't suffer enough." The anger carried by many survivors does not simply vanish when a family member's murderer is executed.

Some of us believe that a sentence of life imprisonment without the possibility of parole is a fate worse than the death penalty. The death penalty brings with it lots of attention, lots of legal process, lots of lawyer visits and trips to court. Hope is possible for a long time. Life without the possibility of parole, after the initial appeals, means life without hope. If the death penalty were abolished and there was no death row, those without the possibility of parole could be

2. In January 2005 six black men and two white men are on death row in Maryland.

segregated, as death row inmates are segregated now.

A new and fascinating voluntary project in the Maryland prison system, conducted by Baltimore's Community Conferencing Center and funded by the Judiciary's Mediation and Conflict Resolution Office (MACRO), creates a facilitated conference between an incarcerated serious offender (rapist or murderer) and the victim or victim's surviving family members. The process creates a safe space where apology and forgiveness are at least possibilities, and has brought relief and healing to many people around the country. We hope the program will be expanded if it continues to be successful in Maryland.

And we cannot forget that the death row inmates' family members are also victims. It is difficult to imagine the agony of Kirk Bloodsworth's family, who knew he was innocent as they waited for the state to execute him. By perpetuating the death penalty, we are perpetuating the protracted suffering of the family members of every death row inmate. They too are in need of healing, and are often included in the conferencing program described above.

Redemption and Violence

Finally, although it is an inquiry that some may find illogical or irrelevant, we also consider the possibility of redemption. Most religions offer some process for purification from sin or some opportunity to change one's life utterly and walk a righteous path. In many religious traditions it is held that the Divinity loves, above all others, a sinner who abandons his wicked ways.

While we do not suggest that redemption absolves one of responsibility for murder or other criminal behavior, we recognize that there are inmates who "see the light," transform their lives and become positive forces inside prisons. This is a foundational concern for some who oppose the death penalty, because they believe the possibility of redemption, or spiritual healing, is always available.

As juxtaposed to a move towards healing, we are sad to note that maintaining the death penalty moves us into bad company. According to Amnesty International, in 2003, four countries were responsible for committing 84 percent of the known executions in the world: China (approximately 726), Iran (approximately 108), the United States (65) and Viet Nam (approximately 64). It gives us pause to consider the possible connection between repression and violence.

And make no mistake, cold-blooded executions are violent acts. Communities, rulers and governments have been carrying them out for a very long time. We have executed by stoning, crucifying, drawing and quartering, burning at the stake, beheading, dunking and drowning, hanging, firing squads, gas chambers, and electrocution.

In Maryland, hangings were conducted in public until 1922, when the Legislature moved executions inside the Maryland Penitentiary to avoid the "curious mobs." In 1955, concern over the cruelty of hangings led the Legislature to switch to performing executions in the gas chamber. In 1993, the state began to execute people by lethal injection.

Some differentiate lethal injection as a departure from former violent forms of execution, calling it humane to "put someone to sleep." This is a matter of debate (although it is clearly a more humane mode of execution for the execution witnesses to observe, as compared with the shaking and charring seen in electric chairs or the grotesque contorted faces in the gas chambers).

In Maryland, people being executed are strapped at the arms, legs and mid-section to a gurney with their arms sticking straight out in the form of a cross (pictures of the execution chamber are posted on the Department of Public Safety and Corrections Web site). Then two IV needles are injected by non-medical personnel (the American Medical Association's Code of Ethics forbids physician participation in, supervision of, or consultation about lethal injections) before the curtain is drawn open to allow a certain six to 12 people to witness the execution.

Three drugs are used. The first is an anesthetic that is supposed to put the condemned person to sleep. The second is a neuromuscular blocking agent, usually Pavulon, that paralyzes the person's muscle system and halts breathing, but does not cause unconsciousness or block pain. The third drug stops the heart.

In his failed legal challenge, Steven Oken, who was executed by lethal injection in Maryland on June 17, 2004, claimed that these drugs mask "excruciating pain." If the short-acting anesthetic fails or wears off, as critics claim it does, Pavulon would prevent those being executed from showing or indicating in any way that they were experiencing the pain and horror of suffocation, and when the third drug is injected, perhaps the pain of cardiac arrest.

Tyrone Gilliam was executed by lethal injection in Maryland on Nov. 16, 1998. He was injected with sodium pentothal, and four minutes later with Pavulon. After some period of time he was injected with potassium chloride and was pronounced dead 13 minutes after the first injection. The state later admitted that there was a leak in the IV line that delivered the anesthetic and deadly chemicals to Gilliam. No one knows what Tyrone Gilliam experienced.

Many botched lethal injection executions have been documented across the country. In some cases it has taken executioners up to an hour to find a good vein, because of scarred veins due to drug use or medical conditions, or because of small veins. In one case a vein collapsed during an execution and the needle popped out, causing the whole procedure to have to be repeated. There have also been equipment failures, like Gilliam's leaking line. Some lethal injections have taken up to a half hour after the first injection to kill the person being injected.

The use of Pavulon and other neuromuscular blocking agents has been condemned as cruel by the American Veterinary Medical Association, which does not allow these drugs to be used to put animals "to sleep." Can we say, with confidence, that a drug deemed too brutal for pet euthanasia is not brutal when used to kill people?

Evolution and "Enough"

Robert M. Morgenthau, who has been Manhattan's District Attorney since 1975, joined many others last week [December 2004] testifying against the death penalty in New York. The *New York Times* reported that the city's top prosecutor quoted George Bernard Shaw to illustrate his own objections to the death penalty.

"It is the deed that teaches, not the name we give it."

Morgenthau said. "The death penalty exacts a terrible price in dollars, lives and human decency. Rather than tamping down the flames of violence, it fuels them."

The American Bar Association has called for a death penalty moratorium. The Catholic Bishops, the International Declaration of Human Rights, Amnesty International and countless other groups have called for abolishing the death penalty. Most of the world, and 12 U.S. states, have evolved beyond this form of state sanctioned violence. It is now time for Maryland to evolve. We will follow the *Burch* case with great interest, and we appeal to the General Assembly to take action.

It is time to say "enough."

"There is more to executions than justice for the dead. There is also protection for the living."

The Death Penalty Protects Innocent People

Jeff Jacoby

Jeff Jacoby in the following viewpoint concedes that the death penalty cannot be totally infallible. Nevertheless, the exacting requirements of due process make death penalty cases extraordinarily error free, he maintains. Consequently, very few, if any, innocent people are executed. Jacoby also argues that imposing the death penalty is just punishment for the most serious crimes. In addition, Jacoby asserts that the deterrent effect of the death penalty prevents the murder of innocent people. Jacoby has been an op-ed columnist for the *Boston Globe* since 1994.

As you read, consider the following questions:

1. What examples does Jacoby use to demonstrate that "no human endeavor is utterly foolproof"?
2. What are the benefits of having the death penalty, in the author's view?
3. What research does Jacoby cite in support of his claim that the execution of murderers saves innocent lives?

Jeff Jacoby, "Executions Saves Innocents," *The Boston Globe*, September 28, 2003, p. H11. Copyright © 2003 by the Globe Newspaper Company. Reproduced by permission of Copyright Clearance Center, Inc.

Governor Mitt Romney has charged a blue-ribbon commission [in 2003] with drafting a death penalty law for Massachusetts that can be applied with 100 percent infallibility. The commission will not be able to do so—no legal instrument can be 100 percent infallible—but I don't blame the governor for wanting it to try. In recent years, anti–death penalty propagandists have succeeded in stoking the fear that capital punishment is being carelessly meted out. But it's a bogus accusation: Of the 875 prisoners executed in the United States in modern times, not one has been retroactively proved innocent. Widely trumpeted claims meant to illustrate the system's sloppiness—that more than 100 innocent men have been freed from Death Row, for example, or that death penalty cases have a 68 percent error rate—fall apart under scrutiny. In fact, so exacting is the due process in these cases that the death penalty in America is probably the most accurately administered criminal sanction in the world.

The propaganda has taken its toll, however. Romney knows that many people who would otherwise support capital punishment now hesitate for fear it may lead to an awful miscarriage of justice. Hence his call for "a standard of proof that is incontrovertible"—an uncompromising benchmark endorsed by members of the new panel. "In this work," says co-chairman Frederick Bieber, a geneticist at Boston's Brigham and Women's Hospital, "there is no room for error."

That is a worthy goal, but it cannot be an absolute criterion. No worthwhile human endeavor is utterly foolproof. Dr. Bieber's hospital would have to shut down its operating rooms if surgeons had to guarantee their infallibility. Even at hospitals as renowned as the Brigham, patients sometimes die on the operating table because of blunders or inadvertence. Is that an argument for abolishing surgery? Should air travel be banned because innocent passengers may lose their lives in crashes? Should the pharmaceutical industry be shut down because the wrong drug or dosage, mistakenly taken or prescribed, can kill?

Benefits Outweigh Risks

To make the perfect the enemy of the good is irrational and counterproductive. The benefits of surgery, air travel, and prescription drugs are enormous—far too valuable to give up even though we know that people will die because of the fallibility of doctors and pilots and people who handle medicine. The same is true of capital punishment: The benefits of a legal system in which judges and juries have the option of sentencing the cruelest or coldest murderers to death far outweigh the potential risk of executing an innocent person. And there is this added reassurance: The risk of an erroneous execution is infinitesimal, and getting smaller all the time.

Justice for the Victim

The justice that the death penalty seeks, it seeks foremostly for the deceased, who can no longer demand it for himself. In another way, the death penalty is society's belated application of self-defense in place of the victim. "We should like to have been there," the sentence says, "to have met lethal force with lethal force for the victim's sake."

The death penalty thus honors and commemorates the dead and speaks to the sanctity of life in the civilized order.

Thomas F. Bertonneau, *The Detroit News*, June 3, 2001. www.detnews.com.

And the benefits? First and foremost, the death penalty makes it possible for justice to be done to those who commit the worst of all crimes. The execution of a murderer sends a powerful moral message: that the innocent life he took was so precious, and the crime he committed so horrific, that he forfeits his own right to remain alive.

When a vicious killer is sent to the electric chair or strapped onto a gurney for a lethal injection, society is condemning his crime with a seriousness and intensity that no other punishment achieves. By contrast, a society that sentences killers to nothing worse than prison—no matter how depraved the killing or how innocent the victim—is a society that doesn't *really* think murder is so terrible.

Protection for the Living

But there is more to executions than justice for the dead. There is also protection for the living. Though Romney didn't say so when he introduced his new commission, the real threat to innocent life is not the availability of the death penalty, but the absence of one. For every time a murderer is executed, innocent lives are saved.

The foes of capital punishment have denied for years that putting murderers to death has a deterrent effect on other potential killers. That has always flown in the face of common sense and history—after all, wherever murder is made punishable by death, murder rates generally decline. But it also flies in the face of a lengthening shelf of research that confirms the death penalty's deterrent effect.

A recent study at the University of Colorado, for instance, finds "a statistically significant relationship between executions, pardons, and homicide. Specifically, each additional execution reduces homicides by five to six." A paper by three Emory University economists concludes: "Our results suggest that capital punishment has a strong deterrent effect. . . . In particular, each execution results, on average, in 18 fewer murders—with a margin of error of plus or minus 10."

Comparable results have been reached by scholars at the University of Houston, SUNY Buffalo, Clemson, and the Federal Communications Commission. All these studies have been published within the past three years [since 2003]. And all of them underscore an inescapable bottom line: The execution of murderers protects innocent life.

"*[The death penalty] is not vengeful, but a just retribution by the State for heinous acts.*"

Executions Deliver Reasonable Retribution

Bob Goodlatte

In the following viewpoint Congressman Bob Goodlatte affirms his support for the death penalty as just retribution for heinous crimes such as those committed by Lee Boyd Malvo and John Allen Mohammed, the Washington, D.C.–area snipers who killed ten people in 2002. Goodlatte maintains that Maryland's 2002 moratorium on the death penalty is a bad idea. In his opinion, fair application of the death penalty is necessary for justice. Bob Goodlatte is a U.S. congressman representing Virginia's Sixth District.

As you read, consider the following questions:

1. According to Goodlatte, what was the response of Maryland public officials to the sniper slayings?
2. Who, in Goodlatte's opinion, ought to set the standards for the death penalty?
3. What efforts does Goodlatte say he has supported in Congress and on the House Judiciary Committee?

Bob Goodlatte, "Weekly Report," www.house.gov/goodlatte, November 1, 2002.

For twenty-two days last month [October 2002] the greater Washington, D.C. area, stretching as far south as Ashland, Virginia, was under siege.[1] Each morning local residents woke up fearful that tragedy had struck again . . . that another innocent life had suddenly been cut short. Shocked families and friends of the victims grieved, school was canceled, sporting events moved to undisclosed locations. Strip malls and gas stations were deserted. Terror gripped the region.

With the recent apprehension of two suspects [Lee Boyd Malvo and John Allen Mohammed], who have since been formally charged in the sniper shootings, there is talk of justice and debate surrounding the death penalty has been revived.

Prior to the sniper case, Maryland had implemented a statewide moratorium on the death penalty. In the aftermath of the shootings, and the discussion surrounding trial jurisdiction, nearly every public official in Maryland has called on prosecutors to pursue the death penalty when exacting judgment on the snipers. The reasoning is that these crimes are so atrocious, the violence so senseless, the murders so abhorrent that the snipers deserve the death penalty. I agree but for some this is a reversal or an exception to a call for a moratorium on the imposition of the death penalty and points out why these broad moratoriums are a bad idea.

The Death Penalty as Just Retribution

All who view the death penalty as a just form of deterrence and retribution would agree, capital punishment should only be used in the most heinous crimes and certainly the cold-blooded anonymous murder of random people on our streets qualifies.

However the standard cannot be set based upon the widespread publicity that a particular case receives or on political expediency but rather on careful standards established by legislatures and courts.

The death penalty is an issue of utmost moral signifi-

1. In October 2002 sniper shots killed ten people and critically injured three others in the Washington, D.C., area. On October 24, Lee Boyd Malvo and John Allen Mohammed were arrested for the crimes. Malvo was convicted of capital murder on December 18, 2003, and given a life term. Mohammed was also convicted, receiving a death sentence in 2004. At the time of publication, he is awaiting execution.

cance. Any discussion goes to the heart of our personal beliefs surrounding justice, retribution, life and death.

The Death Penalty as Retribution: Some Reasons Death Penalty Supporters Give for Favoring the Death Penalty				
Reason	2003 %	2001 %	2000 %	1991 %
An eye for an eye/They took a life/Fits the crime	37	48	40	40
They deserve it	13	6	5	5
Save taxpayers money/ Cost of prison	11	20	12	12
Deterrent for potential crimes/Set an example	11	10	8	8
They will repeat the crime/ Keep them from repeating it	7	6	4	4
Biblical reasons	5	3	3	3
Serve justice	4	1	3	2
Fair punishment	3	1	3	2

Statistics from Jeffrey M. Jones, Gallup Organization, June 3, 2003.

I personally believe that if a defendant is accorded their Constitutional protections and is found guilty by a jury of peers, than the death penalty is just punishment for certain murders.

Societal Standards

Capital punishment sets a societal standard that assaults on human life will not be tolerated. It says that life, innocent life, is precious and that the lives of murderers and victims should not be viewed as morally equivalent. It is not vengeful, but a just retribution by the State for heinous acts and a deterrent to others who might contemplate similar evils.

Those who support the death penalty have a unique responsibility to ensure that it is applied fairly. There would be no greater travesty in justice than if an individual were wrongly executed. In my work in Congress and on the House Judiciary Committee, I have supported efforts to ensure that inmates have access to DNA testing to establish innocence and adequate legal representation.

With the sniper crimes fresh in our minds and the funeral for the final victim having just taken place, it is understandable that there would be a clamoring for justice and even revenge. Suddenly debate surrounding the justness of the death penalty seems completely removed from the reality of these attacks.

The death penalty is needed in our criminal justice system. It must be applied fairly and carefully. But a moratorium sends the wrong message to killers and a moratorium inconsistently applied sets the wrong standard for society.

> *"Retributive justice is fueled by hatred and satisfied only with full and complete revenge—the more cruel, the more satisfying."*

Executions Do Not Deliver Reasonable Retribution

Robert Grant

Robert Grant contends in the following viewpoint that the only motive for demanding the death penalty as opposed to life imprisonment is revenge. Grant argues that the vengeful justice offered by the death penalty is not reasonable. By making revenge possible, the death penalty encourages victims, their families, and society to react to violence violently, thereby making the nation ever more disordered. Grant is a New York attorney and former judge.

As you read, consider the following questions:
1. According to Grant, what is the "crude mathematics" of retributive justice?
2. What evidence does Grant offer that retributive justice does not work and is thus not reasonable?
3. How should offenders be treated, according to Grant, in order to reduce violence in society?

Robert Grant, "Capital Punishment and Violence," *The Humanist*, vol. 64, January/February, 2004, pp. 25–29. Copyright © 2004 by the American Humanist Association. Reproduced by permission of the author.

To understand the debate over capital punishment, it is necessary to identify the purpose of the criminal justice system. To a majority of Americans it is, essentially, to retaliate and punish those who commit crimes, especially brutal and vicious murders, thus balancing the scales of justice. To others its goal is to reduce violence overall. The question of capital punishment, then, pits two great demands of society against each other: the demand for retribution for violating the most basic duty of the social contract—the duty not to murder another—and the need to eliminate, or at least minimize, society's culture of violence. . . .

Retributive Justice Equals Revenge

Many in U.S. society demand vengeance and retribution for violent criminal conduct. Retributive justice means that the criminal must be made to pay for the crime by a crude mathematics that demands the scales of justice be balanced; this appeals to humanity's basest animal instincts and ancient demands for an eye for an eye, a life for a life. Retributive justice is fueled by hatred and satisfied only with full and complete revenge—the more cruel, the more satisfying. Civil liberties defender and lawyer Clarence Darrow observed that the state "continues to kill its victims, not so much to defend society against them . . . but to appease the mob's emotions of hatred and revenge." After Oklahoma City bomber Timothy McVeigh was executed [in 2004] amid wide television coverage, over 80 percent of the viewers polled said that he deserved to die; many said his death was too clinical and he should have died more painfully. One man said that McVeigh should have been stoned to death. Others were willing to forego his execution because they thought that life behind bars with no possibility of parole would be a greater punishment.

Retributive justice has a bad history, however, as it has historically been used to enforce a class society by oppressing the poor and protecting the rich. It has been used to impose racism by applying the law in an unfairly heavy-handed way upon African-American citizens and in a lenient manner upon white Americans. The U.S. justice system has imprisoned more than two million people; about half are black, although African-Americans constitute only 12 percent of the total population. The prison system has been likened to a twenty-first century form of slavery.

More astonishing, perhaps, is that execution statistics from 1977 through 2002 show that capital punishment isn't so much a national problem as it is a problem local to the South. Nationally, 563 executions occurred during this period and the eleven states of the old Confederacy account for about 87.5 percent of these. Texas is way ahead of the pack, having performed about one-third of all executions. In 2002 Texas alone killed thirty-three death row prisoners. It's no coincidence that the South is also the most violent region of the country. However as more and more death row prisoners in other states exhaust their appeals, capital punishment will become more of a national problem. . . .

[T]here is only one purpose, one motive, one true reason for demanding death over life imprisonment: revenge. The issue isn't whether the state has the right to execute those who commit premeditated murder; it has. The issue is whether the state ought to execute convicted murders.

Retributive Justice Is Not Working

The U.S. justice system has reverted to a strictly punitive method in order to prove "tough on crime" and in the hope that stronger punishment will somehow deter future criminal activity. But the reality is that severe punishment isn't working. Kids and petty offenders under the current system become hardened, violent, and persistent criminals. The present punitive and retaliatory justice system is unworthy of the American people's high standard of justice, which values the individual and demands equal justice for all.

Many who seek to eliminate the culture of violence in society assert that capital punishment actually exacerbates the level and intensity of violence in the community. They observe that the state is backwardly killing people in order to teach others not to kill. They search for ways to heal the effects of crime upon society, the victim, and the offender. Restorative justice seeks to eliminate violence from the community and heal the harm done to the extent possible.

Violence is a highly contagious social disease that causes

emotional, psychological, and physical damage and turns a peaceful person into a hostile one. The essence of violence is hatred, anger, rage, and desire for revenge caused by an act of wrongful violence internalized by the victim. When one allows oneself to be filled with these emotions in response to a violent attack, it allows the attacker to do more than just cause physical injuries. The attacker then does emotional and psychological damage as well. She or he has destroyed the victim's sense of inner tranquility and stability—a destruction that remains long after the physical injuries have healed. When anger, rage, hatred, and vengeance fill that space, the victim is turned from a peaceful to a violent person. This violence is the self-inflicted destruction of one's inner peace.

Life Imprisonment as Retribution

I do not believe that it is rational to assign as one of the legitimate goals of a system of punishment the exaction of retribution, in some special fashion or further degree that goes beyond the inherently retributive nature of any system of punishments. Thus, life imprisonment for murder is every bit as retributive as the death penalty for murder, even if it is less severe. Its failure to imitate the crime does not make it less retributive.

Hugo Bedau, *Debating the Death Penalty*, 2004.

And violence begets more violence. It is a contagion spreading hatred, anger, rage, and desire for revenge to others out of empathy for the victim. Moreover, a violent victim may seek revenge against the original perpetrator and can be tempted to take out that anger on family members and friends when emotional triggers enflame the violent condition. Violent people don't have ample social skills to resolve differences peacefully and thus the contagion spreads. Each time a person commits a violent act with the intent to injure or kill, the attacker not only causes physical, emotional, and psychological injury to the victim but becomes a more violent person as well. Every act of violence makes the perpetrator more violent—whether the person is someone assaulting an innocent shopkeeper, acting in self-defense, performing a state execution, or soldiering in war. The contagious nature of violence infects the morally righteous police officer as well as the brutal lawbreaker. In his study of young murderers, Cornell University human development professor James Garbarino observes:

> Epidemics tend to start among the most vulnerable segments of the population and then work their way outward, like ripples in a pond. These vulnerable populations don't cause the epidemic. Rather, their disadvantaged position makes them a good host for the infection. . . . The same epidemic model describes what is happening with boys who kill.

Horrifically, this is a social disorder that can turn innocent people against each other.

A productive way to react to an act of violence is to have the courage to resist the normal impulse for revenge and punishment, to refrain from allowing anger, hatred, rage, and vengeance to destroy one's inner peace. Civil rights activist Martin Luther King Jr. observed:

> Returning violence for violence only multiplies violence, adding deeper darkness to a night already devoid of stars. Darkness cannot drive out darkness, only light can do that. Hate cannot drive out hate; only love can do that.

On the day of McVeigh's execution, a pastor at a memorial service for some of the victims' families asked, "Is there another way we can respond to this violence without doing violence ourselves?" Restorative justice doesn't promote anger, hatred, rage, or revenge by society or by the victim but offers a nonviolent response to the violence done. The focus of restorative justice isn't the punishment of the offender; it is the separation of the violent person from peaceful society for the protection of law-abiding citizens. With a peaceful attitude and conscious decision to choose a nonviolent and nonvengeful response, the cycle of violence can be broken and the contagion stopped. It is all a matter of attitude and the realization that violence should be countered in a mature and rational manner in order to protect society without doing damage to its citizens.

The Disease of Violence

So we need to approach the problem of capital punishment not as a legal matter determining the rights and duties of the parties but as if we were treating a disease—the disease of violence. The past one hundred years have comprised the most violent century in human history. That violence is reflected in our television programs, movies, video games, literature, political attitudes, militaristic paranoia, the alarming abuse toward children, pervasive domestic violence, hostility toward the genuinely poor and helpless, the persistence of racism and intolerance, the way we treat petty juvenile offenders, and the mistreatment of prisoners. When we impose severe and excessive punishment, when we seek an eye for an eye, a tooth for a tooth, a life for a life, when we seek revenge on lawbreakers by some clumsy arithmetic we call justice, we become violent law abiders. We become what we say we abhor—more like criminals—more violent people. And the contagion spreads.

Every time we send a criminal to jail, especially a juvenile offender, it is a failure of society; every time that we execute a murderer, it is another failure of society. Where were the caring family members, helpful friends, concerned teachers, and supportive social workers when that criminal was a child being abused and neglected? Who loved that child? Who educated that child so that he or she could succeed in this world? Who demeaned that child because his or her skin color or religion or ethnicity was different from the majority in the community? Who did violence to that child by relegating him or her to poverty and then hating that child because he or she was poor? Generally speaking, children who are loved and cared for don't become criminals. Family and community violence toward children, including top-down governmental violence, turns some of them into criminals. Ethical communities don't need a police officer on every street corner because ethical communities care for all their children. Criminals aren't born; they are made.

And once made, society gives little thought to rehabilitating the offender, since the purpose of retributive justice is to punish. Or they view punishment as itself rehabilitative. Americans pretend that state-inflicted cruelty will somehow teach a violent felon not to be cruel and violent; and then 97 percent of these "rehabilitated" violent criminals are released into civil society. The theory seems to be that punishment teaches one how to become a good and respected member of the community. Yet the current punishments only succeed in destroying an offender's self-esteem by imprisoning that person and separating him or her from family and friends, then dehumanizing the prisoner by referring to him or her by a number instead of a name. Prisoners also become victims of the internal violence of prison life and, when not building up resentments, become schooled by other inmates in the techniques of crime—aware that society's rejection will continue once they are released.

In order to foster a less violent society, the treatment of the offender should be as humane and non-violent as forcible incarceration can allow. Rehabilitation of the offender ought to be a necessary condition of parole. Life imprisonment without the possibility of parole ought to be the alternative to capital punishment.

Restorative justice seeks to eliminate the culture of violence in U.S. society and replace it with a culture of caring. It's a matter of attitude. We must not allow our hearts to be filled with hatred, anger, rage, and the desire for revenge. It's hard to put aside such feelings when a child or loved one is murdered, especially if the killing is particularly brutal or cruel. This is why violence is so hard to subdue. Look at the difficulties in restoring peace in countries like Northern Ireland, Israel, Bosnia, and India and Pakistan which have engaged in civil wars. Similarly, if we don't find a way to break the cycle of violence we will never be able to end the culture of violence that infects the United States.

Restorative justice doesn't ask that we "turn the other cheek." Restorative justice doesn't seek mercy or forgiveness for those who, by the calculus of duties and rights, deserve to die. Rather, it asks us to protect ourselves from the disease of violence by not killing the despised one. Someone must go first to stop the cycle of violence, the obvious candidate is the state. The words of John Donne from his poem "No Man Is an Island" seem particularly appropriate when we execute a condemned prisoner: "Ask not for whom the bell tolls; it tolls for thee!"

*"Capital punishment is taught in both the
Old Testament and the New Testament."*

The Death Penalty Is Consistent with Religious Ethics

Kerby Anderson

Writing from a Christian perspective, Kerby Anderson maintains in the following viewpoint that in both the Old Testament and the New Testament, God commands the use of the death penalty. Anderson further asserts that Christian support for the death penalty ought to be based on biblical teaching, although Anderson also notes secular justifications such as the deterrent effect of the death penalty. Anderson asserts that state-sanctioned executions are not murder and that human governments are obligated to carry out the death penalty because of God's commandment. Kerby Anderson is the president of Probe Ministries International, a nonprofit Christian media group.

As you read, consider the following questions:

1. According to Anderson, what is the principle of *Lex Talionis*?
2. How does Anderson interpret Jesus's Sermon on the Mount with regard to the death penalty?
3. What three reasons does Anderson give supporting the validity of applying Old Testament law to today's society?

S hould Christians support the death penalty? The answer to that question is controversial. Many Christians feel that the Bible has spoken to the issue, but others believe that the New Testament ethic of love replaces the Old Testament law.

Old Testament Examples

Throughout the Old Testament we find many cases in which God commands the use of capital punishment. We see this first with the acts of God Himself. God was involved, either directly or indirectly, in the taking of life as a punishment for the nation of Israel or for those who threatened or harmed Israel.

One example is the flood of Noah in Genesis 6–8. God destroyed all human and animal life except that which was on the ark. Another example is Sodom and Gomorrah (Gen. 18–19), where God destroyed the two cities because of the heinous sin of the inhabitants. In the time of Moses, God took the lives of the Egyptians' first-born sons (Exod. 11) and destroyed the Egyptian army in the Red Sea (Exod. 14). There were also punishments such as the punishment at Kadesh-Barnea (Num. 13–14) or the rebellion of Korah (Num. 16) against the Jews wandering in the wilderness.

The Old Testament is replete with references and examples of God taking life. In a sense, God used capital punishment to deal with Israel's sins and the sins of the nations surrounding Israel.

The Old Testament also teaches that God instituted capital punishment in the Jewish law code. In fact, the principle of capital punishment even precedes the Old Testament law code. According to Genesis 9:6, capital punishment is based upon a belief in the sanctity of life. It says, "Whoever sheds man's blood by man his blood shall be shed, for in the image of God, He made man."

The Mosaic Law set forth numerous offenses that were punishable by death. The first was murder. In Exodus 21, God commanded capital punishment for murderers. Premeditated murder (or what the Old Testament described as "lying in wait") was punishable by death. A second offense punishable by death was involvement in the occult (Exod. 22; Lev. 20; Deut. 18–19). This included sorcery, divination, acting as a medium, and sacrificing to false gods. Third, capital punishment was to be used against perpetrators of sexual sins such as rape, incest, or homosexual practice.

Within this Old Testament theocracy, capital punishment was extended beyond murder to cover various offenses. While the death penalty for these offenses was limited to this particular dispensation of revelation, notice that the principle in Genesis 9:6 is not tied to the theocracy. Instead, the principle of *Lex Talionis* (a life for a life) is tied to the creation order. Capital punishment is warranted due to the sanctity of life. Even before we turn to the New Testament, we find this universally binding principle that precedes the Old Testament law code.

New Testament Principles

Some Christians believe that capital punishment does not apply to the New Testament and church age.

First we must acknowledge that God gave the principle of capital punishment even before the institution of the Old Testament law code. In Genesis 9:6 we read that "Whoever sheds man's blood by man his blood shall be shed, for in the image of God, He made man." Capital punishment was instituted by God because humans are created in the image of God. The principle is not rooted in the Old Testament theocracy, but rather in the creation order. It is a much broader biblical principle that carries into the New Testament.

Even so, some Christians argue that in the Sermon on the Mount Jesus seems to be arguing against capital punishment. But is He?

In the Sermon on the Mount, Jesus is not arguing against the principle of a life for a life. Rather He is speaking to the issue of our personal desire for vengeance. He is not denying the power and responsibility of the government. In the Sermon on the Mount, Jesus is speaking to individual Christians. He is telling Christians that they should not try to replace the power of the government. Jesus does not deny the power and authority of government, but rather He calls individual Christians to love their enemies and turn the other cheek.

Some have said that Jesus set aside capital punishment in John 8 when He did not call for the woman caught in adultery to be stoned. But remember the context. The Pharisees were trying to trap Jesus between the Roman law and the Mosaic law. If He said that they should stone her, He would break the Roman law. If He refused to allow them to stone her, He would break the Mosaic law (Lev. 20:10; Deut. 22:22). Jesus' answer avoided the conflict: He said that he who was without sin should cast the first stone. Since He did teach that a stone be thrown (John 8:7), this is not an abolition of the death penalty.

In other places in the New Testament we see the principle of capital punishment being reinforced. Romans 13:1–7, for example, teaches that human government is ordained by God and that the civil magistrate is a minister of God. We are to obey government for we are taught that government does not bear the sword in vain. The fact that the Apostle Paul used the image of the sword further supports the idea that capital punishment was to be used by government in the New Testament age as well. Rather than abolish the idea of the death penalty, Paul uses the emblem of the Roman sword to reinforce the idea of capital punishment. The New Testament did not abolish the death penalty; it reinforced the principle of capital punishment.

Capital Punishment and Deterrence

Is capital punishment a deterrent to crime? At the outset, we should acknowledge that the answer to this question should not change our perspective on this issue. Although it is an important question, it should not be the basis for our belief. A Christian's belief in capital punishment should be based upon what the Bible teaches, not on a pragmatic assessment of whether or not capital punishment deters crime.

That being said, however, we should try to assess the effectiveness of capital punishment. Opponents of capital punishment argue that it is not a deterrent, because in some states where capital punishment is allowed the crime rate goes up. Should we therefore conclude that capital punishment is not a deterrent?

First, we should recognize that crime rates have been increasing for some time. The United States is becoming a violent society as its social and moral fabric breaks down. So the increase in the crime rate is most likely due to many other factors and cannot be correlated with a death penalty that has been implemented sparingly and sporadically.

Second, there is some evidence that capital punishment is a deterrent. And even if we are not absolutely sure of its deterrent effect, the death penalty should be implemented. If it is a deterrent, then implementing capital punishment certainly will save lives. If it is not, then we still will have followed biblical injunctions and put convicted murderers to death.

Judaism's Pro–Death Penalty Tradition

The preservation of human dignity requires capital punishment of convicted murderers. The position of Judaism is the opposite of the position espoused by liberals. It is precisely because of man's creation in God's image that capital punishment is declared justified and necessary. Human dignity requires execution of murderers, not compassion for their souls.

Steven Plaut, *Jewish Press*, April 23, 2004. www.jewishpress.com.

In a sense, opponents of capital punishment who argue that it is not a deterrent are willing to give the benefit of the doubt to the criminal rather than to the victim. The poet Hyman Barshay put it this way:

The death penalty is a warning, just like a lighthouse throwing its beams out to sea. We hear about shipwrecks, but we do not hear about the ships the lighthouse guides safely on their way. We do not have proof of the number of ships it saves, but we do not tear the lighthouse down.

If capital punishment is even a potential deterrent, that is a significant enough social reason to implement it.

Statistical analysis by [researcher] Dr. Isaac Ehrlich at the University of Chicago suggests that capital punishment is a deterrent. Although his conclusions were vigorously challenged, further cross-sectional analysis has confirmed his conclusions. His research has shown that if the death penalty is used in a consistent way, it may deter as many as eight murders for every execution carried out. If these numbers are indeed accurate, it demonstrates that capital punishment could be a significant deterrent to crime in our society.

Certainly capital punishment will not deter all crime. Psychotic and deranged killers, members of organized crime, and street gangs will no doubt kill whether capital punishment is implemented or not. A person who is irrational or wants to commit a murder will do so whether capital punishment exists or not. But social statistics as well as logic suggest that rational people will be deterred from murder because capital punishment is part of the criminal code.

Capital Punishment and Discrimination

Many people oppose capital punishment because they feel it is discriminatory. The charge is somewhat curious since most of the criminals that have been executed in the last decade are white rather than black. Nevertheless, a higher percentage of ethnic minorities (African-American, Hispanic-American) are on death row. So is this a significant argument against capital punishment?

First, we should note that much of the evidence for discrimination is circumstantial. Just because there is a higher percentage of a particular ethnic group does not, in and of itself, constitute discrimination. A high percentage of whites playing professional ice hockey or a high percentage of blacks playing professional basketball does not necessarily mean that discrimination has taken place. We need to look beneath the allegation and see if true discrimination is taking place.

Second, we can and should acknowledge that some discrimination does take place in the criminal justice system. Discrimination takes place not only on the basis of race, but on the basis of wealth. Wealthy defendants can hire a battery of legal experts to defend themselves, while poor defendants must rely on a court-appointed public attorney.

Even if we acknowledge that there is some evidence of discrimination in the criminal justice system, does it likewise hold that there is discrimination with regard to capital punishment? The U.S. Solicitor General, in his amicus brief for the case *Gregg vs. Georgia*,[1] argued that sophisticated sociological studies demonstrated that capital punish-

---

1. a 1976 case in which the U.S. Supreme Court ruled that the death penalty is not cruel and unusual punishment

ment showed no evidence of racial discrimination. These studies compared the number of crimes committed with the number that went to trial and the number of guilty verdicts rendered and found that guilty verdicts were consistent across racial boundaries.

But even if we find evidence for discrimination in the criminal justice system, notice that this is not really an argument against capital punishment. It is a compelling argument for reform of the criminal justice system. It is an argument for implementing capital punishment carefully.

We may conclude that we will only use the death penalty in cases where certainty exists (e.g., eyewitness accounts, videotape evidence). But discrimination in the criminal justice system is not truly an argument against capital punishment. At its best, it is an argument for its careful implementation.

In fact, most of the social and philosophical arguments against capital punishment are really not arguments against it at all. These arguments are really arguments for improving the criminal justice system. If discrimination is taking place and guilty people are escaping penalty, then that is an argument for extending the penalty, not doing away with it. Furthermore, opponents of capital punishment candidly admit that they would oppose the death penalty even if it were an effective deterrent. So while these are important social and political issues to consider, they are not sufficient justification for the abolition of the death penalty.

Objections to Capital Punishment

One objection to capital punishment is that the government is itself committing murder. Put in theological terms, doesn't the death penalty violate the sixth commandment, which teaches "Thou shalt not kill?"

First, we must understand the context of this verse. The verb used in Exodus 20:13 is best translated "to murder." It is used 49 times in the Old Testament, and it is always used to describe premeditated murder. It is never used of animals, God, angels, or enemies in battle. So the commandment is not teaching that all killing is wrong; it is teaching that murder is wrong.

Second, the penalty for breaking the commandment was

death (Exod. 21:12; Num. 35:16–21). We can conclude therefore that when the government took the life of a murderer, the government was not itself guilty of murder. Opponents of capital punishment who accuse the government of committing murder by implementing the death penalty fail to see the irony of using Exodus 20 to define murder but ignoring Exodus 21, which specifically teaches that government is to punish the murderer.

A second objection to capital punishment questions the validity of applying the Old Testament law code to today's society. After all, wasn't the Mosaic Law only for the Old Testament theocracy? There are a number of ways to answer this objection.

First, we must question the premise. There is and should be a relationship between Old Testament laws and modern laws. We may no longer be subject to Old Testament ceremonial law, but that does not invalidate God's moral principles set down in the Old Testament. Murder is still wrong. Thus, since murder is wrong, the penalty for murder must still be implemented.

Second, even if we accept the premise that the Old Testament law code was specifically and uniquely for the Old Testament theocracy, this still does not abolish the death penalty. Genesis 9:6 precedes the Old Testament theocracy, and its principle is tied to the creation order. Capital punishment is to be implemented because of the sanctity of human life. We are created in God's image. When a murder occurs, the murderer must be put to death. This is a universally binding principle not confined merely to the Old Testament theocracy.

Third, it is not just the Old Testament that teaches capital punishment. Romans 13:1–7 specifically teaches that human government is ordained by God and that we are to obey government because government does not bear the sword in vain. Human governments are given the responsibility to punish wrongdoers, and this includes murderers who are to be given the death penalty.

Finally, capital punishment is never specifically removed or replaced in the Bible. While some would argue that the New Testament ethic replaces the Old Testament ethic, there is no instance in which a replacement ethic is introduced. As we have already seen, Jesus and the disciples never disturb the Old Testament standard of capital punishment. The Apostle Paul teaches that we are to live by grace with one another, but also teaches that we are to obey human government that bears the sword. Capital punishment is taught in both the Old Testament and the New Testament.

"Gut-level reactions may cry out for vengeance, but Jesus' example in the Gospels invites all to develop a new and different attitude toward violence."

The Death Penalty Is Not Consistent with Religious Ethics

Kenneth R. Overberg

Kenneth R. Overberg summarizes the U.S. Catholic bishops' position on the death penalty in the following viewpoint. According to the author, the bishops teach that the death penalty is inconsistent with Christian values and that scripture supports the bishops' opposition to the death penalty. Overberg claims that the Bible urges nonviolence. Kenneth R. Overberg is a professor at Xavier University in Cincinnati, Ohio.

As you read, consider the following questions:
1. What four Christian values does the author assert would be promoted by the abolition of the death penalty?
2. What five death penalty problems does the author cite?
3. What is the focus of Jesus's life and teachings, according to Overberg?

Kenneth R. Overberg, "The Death Penalty: Why the Church Speaks a Counter-culture Message," *Catholic Update*, 2005. Reproduced by permission of St. Anthony Messenger Press and Franciscan Communications.

If someone murdered your child or closest friend, what punishment would you want for the criminal? If you were simply asked your opinion about capital punishment, how would you respond? What reasons would you give for your answer?

Recent polls [in 2005] show that 75 percent of U.S. citizens favor the death penalty. Yet the U.S. Catholic bishops, along with many other Christians and Jews, have spoken out against capital punishment. Beyond polls and statements, powerful scenes dramatize opposing viewpoints: people protesting a death sentence with candlelight vigils, while others gather as if at a party shouting, "Kill the scum!"

This [viewpoint] considers these profound differences in our society, summarizes the teaching of the U.S. bishops and tells a mother's true story of horror and reconciliation after the murder of her daughter.

Gut Level Response vs. Good Moral Decisions

In 1966, less than half of the U.S. population approved of the death penalty. Now polls indicate that about 75 percent approve. Why this dramatic change in public opinion? Certainly, a major factor is the increasing fear and frustration concerning violent crime. Something must be done! Many people turn to the death penalty as a possible remedy. Not only has the public turned in favor of capital punishment, but the U.S. government has also recommended that many more crimes be punishable by the death penalty. This renewed approval reflects traditional reasons for supporting the death penalty: deterrence and retribution. Some who support capital punishment do so because they judge that the threat of death will prevent people from committing crimes. Others judge that some crimes are so horrible that the only appropriate punishment is death.

Those people who oppose the death penalty, however, challenge these traditional reasons. They point out that there is no solid evidence that the death penalty serves as a deterrent. Indeed, they note, examples point in the opposite direction: Some countries that have eliminated the death penalty have had decreasing rates of violent crime, and some death-penalty states have had increasing rates of homicide.

Supporters of capital punishment counter with the argument that the death penalty would be more effective as a deterrent were it not for the many appeals, long delays and limited numbers of those actually executed.

Similar debates surround the issue of retribution. Opponents of capital punishment claim that there is no place in a civilized society for justifying death in terms of retribution. They judge such action to be closer to sheer revenge. They doubt that death can be a means of balancing the disturbed equilibrium of justice that resulted from the original crime. Again, supporters counter with the claim that society will not respect the law unless society's sense of justice is satisfied by the criminal's death.

Other supporters claim that retribution is self-justifying, simply a return in kind. Some justify retribution by appealing to the Bible: "[Y]ou shall give life for life, eye for eye, tooth for tooth . . . ". Scripture scholars tell us that the eye-for-eye mandate is actually an attempt to limit violence in early Hebrew culture. As we know from experience, violence tends to escalate: If you cut off my finger, I retaliate by cutting off your hand. Eye for eye reduced such escalation. As we will see later . . . , eye for eye must be considered in the context of the whole Bible.

Many people have made up their minds about the death penalty without really thinking out its moral implications. They then find and use studies, statistics and stories to fit their conclusions. Could this be true for you? If so, you—and all who are willing to wrestle with this issue—will have to look behind the convictions and be open to developing a new attitude. One's gut-level response may be very strong, but it doesn't necessarily lead to good moral decisions.

Teaching of the U.S. Bishops

The Catholic bishops of the United States have provided careful guidance about this difficult issue, applying the teaching of the universal Church to our American culture. Along with the leadership assemblies of many Churches (for example: American Baptists, Disciples of Christ, Episcopalians, Lutherans, Presbyterians), the U.S. bishops have expressed their opposition to the death penalty. First articulated in 1974, the bishops' position is explained in a 1980 statement, *Capital Punishment*. Individual bishops and state conferences of bishops have repeated in numerous teachings their opposition to the death penalty.

In their 1980 statement, the bishops begin by noting that punishment, "since it involves the deliberate infliction of evil on another," must be justifiable. They acknowledge that the Christian tradition has for a long time recognized a government's right to protect its citizens by using the death penalty in some serious situations. The bishops ask, however, if capital punishment is still justifiable in the present circumstances in the United States.

In this context, the bishops enter the debate about deterrence and retribution. They acknowledge that capital punishment certainly prevents the criminal from committing more crimes, yet question whether it prevents others from doing so. Similarly, concerning retribution, the bishops support the arguments against death as an appropriate form of punishment. The bishops add that reform is a third reason given to justify punishment, but it clearly does not apply in the case of capital punishment. And so they affirm: "We believe that in the conditions of contemporary American society, the legitimate purposes of punishment do not justify the imposition of the death penalty."

Christian Values and the Death Penalty

As with the debate in our wider society, it is important to move behind the discussion of deterrence and retribution to get to the heart of the bishops' position. The statement does just that, by discussing four related values that would be promoted by the abolition of the death penalty.

First, "abolition sends a message that we can break the cycle of violence, that we need not take life for life, that we can envisage more humane and more hopeful and effective responses to the growth of violent crime." The bishops recognize that crime is rooted in the complex reality of contemporary society, including those "social conditions of poverty and injustice which often provide the breeding grounds for serious crime." More attention should go to correcting the root causes of crime than to enlarging death row.

Second, "abolition of capital punishment is also a manifestation of our belief in the unique worth and dignity of each person from the moment of conception, a creature made in the image and likeness of God." This belief, rooted in Scripture and consistently expressed in the social teachings of the Church, applies to all people, including those who have taken life.

Christian Reconciliation

I lost my father and my grandmother to violence, yet I cannot accept the judgment that their killers deserved to be executed. . . . Sometimes, I struggle with my feelings of anger, but then I remember that my father was a Christian minister who preached a message of forgiveness and non-violence.

Bernice King, speech at Ss. Monica and Luke Church, Gary, IN, June 5, 1993.

Third, "abolition of the death penalty is further testimony to our conviction, a conviction which we share with the Judaic and Islamic traditions, that God is indeed the Lord of life." And so human life in all its stages is sacred, and human beings are called to care for life, that is, to exercise good stewardship and not absolute control. The bishops recognize that abortion, euthanasia and the death penalty are not the same issue, but they each point to the same fundamental value: safeguarding the sanctity of life.

Fourth, "we believe that abolition of the death penalty is most consonant with the example of Jesus." In many ways this final point summarizes the other three: the God revealed in the life of Jesus is a God of forgiveness and redemption, of love and compassion—in a word, a God of life. The heart of the bishops' position on the death penalty, then, is found in the gospel.

Gut-level reactions may cry out for vengeance, but Jesus' example in the Gospels invites all to develop a new and different attitude toward violence. The bishops encourage us to embody Jesus' message in practical and civic decisions.

Prisons, Victims, and More

While the gospel leads the bishops to oppose the death penalty, they also recognize the need society has to protect itself. Imprisonment will be necessary, but ought not to dehumanize the convicts. The bishops summarize what they have developed in other documents: Significant changes in the prison system are necessary to make it truly conducive to reform and rehabilitation.

In their statement on capital punishment, the bishops express special concern for the victims of violent crime and their families. "Our society should not flinch from contemplating the suffering that violent crime brings to so many when it destroys lives, shatters families and crushes the hope of the innocent." Care for victims must be given in practical ways, such as financial assistance, pastoral care, medical and psychological treatment.

Some other difficulties directly related to the death penalty, which the statement mentions, are: 1) the death penalty removes the possibility of reform and rehabilitation; 2) there is the possibility of putting an innocent person to death; 3) carrying out the death penalty causes anguish not only for the convict's loved ones but also for the executioners and the witnesses; 4) executions attract great publicity, much of it unhealthy; 5) there is legitimate concern that criminals are sentenced to death in a discriminatory way: It is a reasonable judgment that racist attitudes and the social consequences of racism have some influence in determining who is sentenced to die in our society. Adequate legal representation is an issue that puts poor people at a disadvantage. For many reasons, especially the message of Jesus, the U.S. bishops favor ending the death penalty.

Scripture and the Death Penalty

The Bible is often mentioned in debates about the death penalty. Supporters quote the Exodus passage, eye for eye, while opponents appeal to Ezekiel. "As I live, says the Lord God, I swear I take no pleasure in the death of the wicked man, but rather in the wicked man's conversion, that he may live." In fact, such use of the Bible (finding a "proof text" to affirm one's point of view) is inappropriate.

Scripture scholars teach us to understand the Bible (and its individual books) in historical context: when it was written and why. Thus considered, there is an ambivalence about capital punishment in the Scriptures.

Clearly, the Hebrew Scriptures allowed the death penalty (for a much longer list of offenses than our society would be comfortable with—for example, striking or cursing a parent, adultery, idolatry). Yet, as we see in Ezekiel and many other passages, there is also an attempt to limit violence and to stress mercy. In the Christian Scriptures, Jesus' life and teachings . . . focus on mercy, reconciliation and redemption. (It may also be instructive to recall that Jesus' death was itself an application of the death penalty.) The basic thrust of the Gospels supports opposition to the death penalty.

Indeed, the early Church . . . generally found taking human life to be incompatible with the gospel. Christians were not to participate in capital punishment. Later, after Christianity became the religion of the Roman Empire, opposition to the death penalty declined. Augustine recognized the death penalty as a means of deterring the wicked and protecting the innocent. In the Middle Ages, Thomas Aquinas reaffirmed this position.

The new *Catechism of the Catholic Church* reflects this tradition, stating that the death penalty is possible in cases of extreme gravity. However, the *Catechism* adds: "If bloodless means [that is, other than killing] are sufficient to defend human lives against an aggressor and to protect public order and the safety of persons, public authority should limit itself to such means, because they better correspond to the concrete conditions of the common good and are more in conformity to the dignity of the human person". Clearly, then, the bishops' opposition to the death penalty is in accord with universal Church teaching.

A Mother's Story

Despite the message of Jesus and the teachings of the bishops, many people may still be caught up in the anger and outrage over violent crime. Scriptures and teachings seem so remote; debates over deterrence and retribution prove nothing. For all, but especially for those who feel this way, the following true story may be especially challenging.

Marietta Jaeger and her family were on a camping vacation in Montana when her seven-year-old daughter, Susie, was kidnapped. Searches by the FBI and local authorities turned up nothing. Jaeger describes her initial feelings about the kidnapper: "I could kill him. I meant it with every fiber of my being. I'm sure I could have done it with my bare hands and a smile on my face. I felt it was a matter of justice."

Months passed with no new clues, except a few calls from the kidnapper offering to exchange Susie for a ransom—but the kidnapper never made a specific offer. During this time Jaeger "argued and argued with God," and then "gave God permission to change my heart." Jaeger also began to pray for the kidnapper, acknowledging that "my Christian upbringing and my knowledge of good psychological health had taught me that forgiveness was not an option, but a mandate."

Fifteen months after Susie's kidnapping, the kidnapper was arrested. Although the death penalty was applicable in the case, Jaeger asked the FBI to settle for the alternative, life imprisonment with psychiatric care. Only then did the kidnapper, a young man, finally admit to the rape, strangulation death, decapitation and dismemberment of Susie (within a week of the kidnapping). A short time later, the young man committed suicide.

Jaeger recognizes the need for society to protect itself. "I do not advocate forgiveness for violent people and then release to the streets. I know that there are people who should be separated in a humanely secured manner from the community for the protection of all."

And, of course, she knows intimately the feelings of the victim's family. She understands the desire for revenge, but claims that those who retain an attitude of vindictiveness are tormented, embittered people who have no peace of mind. The quality of their lives is diminished and, in effect, they have given the offender another victim. Jaeger states that the death penalty does not do for the victims' family what they had hoped, but leaves them "empty, unsatisfied and unhealed." She adds, "There is no number of retaliatory deaths which would compensate to me the inestimable value of my daughter's life, nor would they restore her to my arms.". . .

Consistent Ethic of Life

Marietta Jaeger's profoundly moving story is a striking embodiment of Jesus' message and the bishops' recent teachings. Her life—and the lives of so many others like her—is also a dramatic reminder that the ideal can be lived in the real world. Much in our culture—fears, political platforms, media events—promotes a different message. Jaeger's witness, however, challenges all of us to move beyond brutalization to develop a consistent ethic of life, to appreciate the sanctity of all life. . . .

But it all starts with developing a new attitude about violence, an attitude rooted in the countercultural message of the gospel.

Periodical Bibliography

The following articles have been selected to supplement the diverse views presented in this chapter.

American Civil Liberties Union	"The Death Penalty: Questions and Answers," April 29, 2005. www.aclu.org.
John H. Blume and Sheri Lynn Johnson	"Limiting Religious Arguments in Capital Cases," *A Call for Reckoning: Religion and the Death Penalty*, Pew Forum, 2001. www. pewforum.org.
Paul G. Cassell	"We're Not Executing the Innocent," *Wall Street Journal*, June 16, 2000.
Daily Free Press Online Edition	"Death Penalty Verdict Right Step," November 26, 2003. www.dailyfreepress.com.
Ronald Eisenberg	"'Innocence' and the Death Penalty," *Pennsylvania District Attorneys Association Newsletter*, April 2004. www.prodeathpenalty. com.
Bob Enyart	"God's Criminal Justice System," 2000. www. theologyonline.com.
Gregory Kane	"To Murder Victims' Families, Executing Killers Is Justice," *Baltimore Sun.com*, February 5, 2003. www.baltimoresun.com.
Legal Times	"Pushing for an End to Juvenile Executions," September 27, 2004.
Joshua Levinson	"The Truth Behind Capital Punishment," *Daily Campus*, February 3, 2004. www.dailycampus.com.
David Lindorff	"Unjust Executions," *Salon.com*, May 6, 2003. www.salon.com.
National Catholic Reporter	"Ryan Did the Right Thing—Justice," January 24, 2003.
Robert Pambianco	"The Guilty Are Being Executed: Red Herrings from the Anti–Death Penalty Squad," *National Review Online*, June 23, 2000. www.nationalreview.com.
Dale S. Recinella	"No to the Death Penalty," *America*, November 1, 2004.
Amy White	"Religion Far from Unified on Executions," *Modesto Bee*, December 18, 2004.

CHAPTER 2

Does the Death Penalty Deter Crime?

Chapter Preface

For many Americans, the most important purpose of the death penalty is to deter crime. The number of people who believe that the death penalty lowers murder rates is dropping, however. In June 1991 the Gallup Poll Organization polled Americans on the following question: "Do you feel that the death penalty acts as a deterrent to the commitment of murder, that it lowers the murder rate, or not?" Fifty-one percent of those responding said that the death penalty deterred crime while 41 percent said that it did not. Eight percent were undecided. The Gallup Poll Organization asked the same question in May 2004, and at that time 35 percent of the respondents felt that the death penalty deterred crime, while 62 percent said that it did not. Only 3 percent had no opinion.

Ironically, at the same time that public belief in the deterrent effect of the death penalty was dropping in the early years of the twenty-first century, economists were conducting studies that claimed to quantitatively and definitively demonstrate that executions did indeed save lives. Researchers such as Joanna Shepherd, H. Naci Mocan, and R. Kaj Gittings used what is known as the "econometric" method, a combination of statistics and economic theory, to demonstrate that as many as 812 lives could be saved by a single execution. At the same time, much of the congressional testimony offered in support of expanding the USA PATRIOT Act—which enhances law enforcement powers to fight terrorism—to include additional death penalty sentencing for terrorist crimes referenced the "deterrent effect" as justification for changes in U.S. law.

Opponents of the death penalty, however, were quick to point out what they saw as flaws in the econometric method. Columbia law professor Jeffrey Fagan, for example, testifying before the New York State Assembly on January 21, 2005, asserted, "These new studies are fraught with technical and conceptual errors." He cited statistical analysis problems, missing data, small sample size, and a failure "to consider . . . relevant factors that drive murder rates." Death penalty opponents produced statistics of their own, demonstrating the so-called "brutalizing effect" of the death penalty. They attempted to show statistically that rather than dropping in response to executions, the number of murders rose in states that had the death penalty. Furthermore, many experts on terrorism argued that expanding the death penalty to include all terrorist acts might actually have a "reverse deterrent effect." They reasoned that terrorists, who crave publicity for their causes, might actually be encouraged to commit terrorist acts if the death penalty were the sentence for such crimes. As Jessica Stern writes in the *New York Times*, "A terrorist's greatest weapon is popular support. . . . We must not make martyrs out of murderers."

Deterrence is a thorny issue in the death penalty debate, one that sharply divides lawyers, judges, scholars, and politicians. The writers in this chapter discuss how statistics and other measures help experts analyze the deterrent effect of capital punishment.

"It contradicts all human experience to argue that the death penalty does not deter murder."

Common Sense Proves That the Death Penalty Deters Crime

Richard A. Devine

In the following viewpoint Richard A. Devine argues that the death penalty is necessary for deterrence. He discounts the value of statistical studies for making this claim, however, preferring to appeal to common sense. He contends that human behavior changes when faced with certain consequences; thus, when faced with the certainty that they will face death if they commit certain crimes, criminals will often elect not to go through with them. Devine further argues that the death penalty deters felons already in jail from killing each other and members of the prison staff; they would rather be incarcerated for life than face the death penalty, he notes. Richard A. Devine is the state's attorney of Cook County, Illinois.

As you read, consider the following questions:

1. Why is resolving the death penalty debate through statistics unhelpful, according to Devine?
2. In the author's opinion, in what cases is the death penalty necessary for true punishment?
3. What types of murder necessitate the death penalty, according to Devine?

Richard A. Devine, "A Statement on the Death Penalty in Illinois," www.states attorney.org, April 30, 2003.

Those who debate the deterrent value of capital punishment frequently attempt to resolve the issue through statistics. This is unhelpful on several levels. First, social scientists admit that statistical surveys do not establish a cause-effect relationship; they only show correlations. If the death penalty is abolished and homicides drop, a survey will not establish whether abolition caused murder to fall, the penalty was abolished because murder was falling, or the abolition coincided with independent phenomena, such as an aging population, which caused the murder rate to fall.

Second, murder rates are related to multiple variables, many of which will be omitted from most surveys. There are many factors, including gun laws, the size of youth cohorts, migration patterns in cities, crime clearance patterns and the like, which can affect murder rates. There are also many methodological variables affecting the survey's reliability. Ultimately, every survey will be subject to endless impeachment by social scientists who disagree with its results.

Deterrence Among the Incarcerated

However, because the issue of deterrence cannot be resolved one way or another by studies does not mean that it isn't a relevant consideration in the death penalty debate. Capital punishment is necessary for deterrence to the same extent, and in the same cases, where it is necessary for true punishment. Again, we confront those convicts who cannot be punished through imprisonment because they are already serving life imprisonment or equivalent long sentences of incarceration. These convicts include convicted killers and others who are the most violent criminals alive. If we abolish capital punishment, there will be no deterrent to keep these convicts from killing prison staff or fellow prisoners. Again, unsanctioned murder becomes sanctioned killing.

If we impose no death penalty for murder by these inmates, we abandon the attempt to deter murder by them in the penitentiary. We would surrender sovereignty over a population of potential victims and killers in the institution where sovereignty should be strongest.

Every violent felon faces a potential penitentiary sentence when he commits a rape, armed robbery or kidnapping.

When that felon weighs the lives of the victim, the witnesses or the police against the penitentiary, the law must give him a reason to value their lives as much as his own freedom. This will only happen if the criminal knows that he puts his own life in jeopardy when he kills any of them.

There are other criminals who would commit murders where there is only a small likelihood of capture. Some of these criminals molest and hurt very small, defenseless children. Serial thrill killers hunt humans and do not leave the usual clues (personal relationships, geographic proximity, motives, etc.) that otherwise raise the probability of apprehension in any single murder. John Gacy was such a killer. The threat of death is necessary to inject a level of concern into their calculations.

If we refuse to answer these murders with the possibility of the death penalty, we will surrender the law's sovereignty on the streets and in the courtrooms, not just in the penitentiary. Where capital punishment is the only meaningful means of deterrence, the law must defend innocent citizens.

Capital punishment is necessary where it is the only means by which we can attempt to deter murder. But stressing the value of attempting deterrence should not serve to obscure the fact that capital punishment can provide it.

Common Sense

It contradicts all human experience to argue that the death penalty does not deter murder. The fact that murders are still committed does not show a failure of deterrence; it only shows that some murders were not deterred. Every day human beings adjust their behavior in countless ways (e.g., looking before crossing streets, avoiding electrical shocks, wearing seatbelts, washing hands, taking the stairs instead of jumping out the window) to avoid threats of death. It defies common sense to suggest that human nature changes when the threat of death is capital punishment.

Any threat of punishment will deter some criminal activity. The penitentiaries are full of guilty criminals, yet there is still crime. Yet, no one would abolish the penitentiary for failing to deter crime. The penitentiary deters crime because it punishes those who are not deterred.

Common sense informs us that most people would prefer to remain out of jail, that the threat of public humiliation is enough to deter some people, that a sentence of twenty years will deter most people more than a sentence of two years, that a life sentence will deter most would-be criminals more than a sentence of twenty years. I think that we have common-sense evidence that the death penalty is a better deterrent than prison sentences. For one thing, as Richard Herrnstein and James Q. Wilson have argued in *Crime and Human Nature*, a great deal of crime is committed on a cost-benefit schema, wherein the criminal engages in some form of risk assessment as to his or her chances of getting caught and punished in some manner. If he or she estimates the punishment mild, the crime becomes inversely attractive, and vice versa. The fact that those who are condemned to death do everything in their power to get their sentences postponed or reduced to long-term prison sentences, in a way lifers do not shows that they fear death more than life in prison.

Louis P. Pojman and Jeffrey Reiman, *The Death Penalty: For and Against*, 1998.

There is a new argument against capital punishment that would finesse the debate by suggesting that life imprisonment is worse than the death penalty. It speaks volumes that the only people pushing this argument are death penalty foes. Its lack of merit is further evidenced by the reality that virtually all condemned prisoners fight to avoid death even when the alternative is life imprisonment. . . .

Some Murders Demand the Death Penalty

The threat of capital punishment is needed for some types of murders. As discussed earlier, capital punishment must be available to ensure punishment and deterrence in the following types of murders: repeat murders, mass murders, felony murders, murders to evade apprehension or prosecution (including murders of police officers and witnesses), and murders by inmates.

Society should also consider the penalty for murders where the likelihood of apprehension and conviction is especially low and the victims are distinctly vulnerable. These murders include those of the very young, the elderly, and the disabled.

These lists are not intended to be exhaustive. They only identify murder cases where capital punishment is a necessity.

On the other hand, we have codified some categories of death penalty murders in response to particular cases. Illinois currently has categories of capital murders that are based upon the offenses of armed violence, calculated criminal drug conspiracies, and vehicular hijackings, as well as homicides of drug kingpins. These categories of death penalty cases should be repealed. Keeping unneeded death penalty provisions can only increase the danger of future injustice.

"A former client of mine, a convicted murderer, once said, 'You can tell people that you're going to boil 'em in hot oil, but it won't deter crime. . . .'"

Common Sense Proves That the Death Penalty Does Not Deter Crime

Marshall Dayan

In the following viewpoint Marshall Dayan argues that the death penalty does not deter crime because most criminals do not believe they will get caught. To illustrate, Dayan discusses a real-life example. Even in this case, where the offender knew beforehand what punishment he would receive for committing the crime, he went through with it anyway, figuring he would get away with it. Dayan is a law professor at North Carolina Central University.

As you read, consider the following questions:
1. What are punishment's four purposes, in Dayan's view?
2. What must happen for deterrence to work, according to Dayan?
3. Who is William G. Huggins, and why does his case demonstrate that the death penalty does not deter crime?

How often have we heard politicians, prosecutors and others insist that we as a society must impose the death penalty for the crime of murder because it will certainly deter others from committing a similar crime? It is a familiar refrain, and we hear it even more lately as a defense to those who propose that a moratorium on the death penalty is necessary to attempt to fix the numerous problems plaguing application of the death penalty—the shocking number of innocent people sentenced to death, questions of race and class discrimination, the uneven and arbitrary quality of counsel, the politics of the judiciary presiding over capital trials and appeals, and the absence of narrow guidelines for who might be eligible for this most severe punishment.

Yet, a recent news event here in North Carolina has once again called into question whether even the death penalty can actually deter crime.

Four Purposes of Punishment

Among the main purposes of punishment for crime are deterrence, prevention, rehabilitation and retribution. Of these four, deterrence is considered the most important, because theoretically it can have the greatest effect on society. Numerous social science studies, however, have called into question whether the death penalty is any more effective at deterring crime than is imprisonment for life.

In spite of these studies, prosecutors regularly justify the use of the death penalty by insisting that the death penalty does deter crime. Others argue that no criminal punishment can deter very much, not even the death penalty, because for deterrence to work, the potential criminal must think about the consequences. A former client of mine, a convicted murderer, once said, "You can tell people that you're going to boil 'em in hot oil, but it won't deter crime, because criminals don't think they're going to get caught."

Similarly, Justice William Brennan wrote: "It is not denied that many, and probably most, capital crimes cannot be deterred by the threat of punishment. Thus the argument can apply only to those who think rationally about the commission of capital crimes. Particularly is that true when the potential criminal, under this argument, must not only consider the risk of punishment, but also distinguish between two possible punishments. The concern, then, is with a particular type of potential criminal, the rational person who will commit a capital crime knowing that the punishment is long-term imprisonment, which may well be for the rest of his life, but will not commit the crime knowing that the punishment is death. On the face of it, the assumption that such persons exist is implausible."

The Most Likely to Be Deterred

While Justice Brennan is probably right that no such person exists, it is possible to think of who such a person might be. The criminal subject to deterrence surely would know that the death penalty could be applied to his crime if he were to be caught, and would therefore have to have some legal knowledge. This person would also know the likelihood of being caught, and would therefore have to have some knowledge of law enforcement. In short, the person most likely to be deterred by the threat of the death penalty would be a prosecutor, a district attorney or assistant district attorney.

A Disturbing Conclusion

I prefer life-without-parole sentences to the death penalty because capital punishment has a corrosive influence on any society, and there is no evidence that the death penalty really does anything to fight crime. In fact, a recent study commissioned by *The New York Times* examined FBI data and found that death-penalty states' average murder rates consistently exceeded those of non-death-penalty states. The study reached the very disturbing conclusion that, over the last twenty years, death-penalty states' homicide rates have been, on a per capita basis, an astonishing 48 percent to 101 percent higher than in non-death-penalty states. Of America's twelve non-death-penalty states, ten have murder rates that are below—often far below—the national average.

John D. Bessler, *Phi Kappa Phi Forum*, Winter 2002.

Recently, Assistant District Attorney William G. Huggins Jr. of the Lee County judicial district was arrested on charges of solicitation of murder. If the murder had taken place, Huggins could have been convicted for acting in concert to commit first-degree murder or accessory before the fact to first-degree murder, either of which could carry the death penalty.

A Lee County District Court judge found probable cause to believe that the crime of solicitation had been committed, and bound the case over to the Superior Court. If anyone could be deterred by the threat of the death penalty, it would be a prosecutor. In particular, it would be an assistant district attorney in the Lee County prosecutorial district. The elected district attorney, Thomas Lock, has frequently sought the death penalty in this prosecutorial district, so the death penalty is in no way foreign to William Huggins. Yet if the allegations are true, Huggins was undeterred. Those who argue that the death penalty has a deterrent effect simply haven't heard about William G. Huggins Jr.

"*Until now, believers in the deterrence effect of executions have had little hard evidence with which to [make their case]. . . . But there now come impressive new findings.*"

Studies Show That the Death Penalty Deters Crime

Iain Murray

In the following viewpoint Iain Murray reports on a new study showing that the death penalty deters murders. He applauds the study, claiming that it is a convincing defense of capital punishment. Although he expresses some reservations about a few odd results, he nonetheless argues that this research is an important contribution to the death penalty debate. Currently a senior fellow at the Competitive Enterprise Institute, Murray is a prolific writer on science, technology, and social issues.

As you read, consider the following questions:
1. According to Murray, what has intensified the public debate over the death penalty?
2. How many innocent lives do researchers Hashem Dezhbakhsh, Paul Rubin, and Joanna Mehlhop Shepherd say will be saved per execution?
3. In his viewpoint, Murray notes three odd results in the study by the Emory researchers. What are they?

Europe assails us as barbaric for embracing it. Churchmen worry for our immortal souls because we think that it is just. Governors lose sleep over the issue. It is the death penalty, and the debate over its imposition is now more intense than at any time since its brief suspension as unconstitutional in the 1970s. The federal executions [in 2001] of terrorist Timothy McVeigh and drug kingpin Juan Raul Garza, the first uses of the punishment by federal authorities since 1963, have intensified the arguments on both sides. European governments used the issue as a stick with which to beat President [George W.] Bush during his first visit to the Continent, and in Ohio, a group of religious-conservative lawmakers have stood up to oppose the penalty based on their religious faith.

In this atmosphere, death penalty proponents have found their arguments tested as never before. The contention that it is a just punishment is countered by the possibility that innocents have been executed. Although there is no proof that such a calamity has occurred since the restoration of the death penalty in 1976, its mere potential has been enough for some state governors to impose moratoria on executions. The argument that the penalty at least incapacitates the murderer himself and prevents him from murdering again has been attacked by life-imprisonment advocates as an overreaction. Murderers are the least likely of all criminals to repeat their crime, but it does occur. One notable . . . case occurred in June 1999, when Leroy Schmitz, who served eleven years in a Massachusetts prison for strangling his girlfriend, murdered his wife in similar fashion in Montana. But for the most part, murderers who kill again have not been found guilty of capital murder and have never faced the death sentence.

The deterrent effect of execution, the argument that might serve death penalty proponents best, has had the worst time of all. A *USA Today* poll carried out in early June [2001], around the time of McVeigh's execution, found that 66 percent of respondents did not think that his death would serve as "a deterrent to future acts of violence and murder." Major figures in the debate, such as former governor of New York Mario Cuomo, point to cases such as that of Andrea Yates, who admitted slaying her five children, as evidence that many murders are irrational acts and therefore cannot be deterred. Others have argued that there are too few executions to have any deterrent effect. The *Chicago Tribune* editorialized on June 10th [2001], "If we wanted the death penalty to deter future criminals, we would impose it the way China does: far more often, and with far less evidence. Or we would apply it to all kinds of offenses the way we did in low-crime colonial times, when Virginians could be executed for stealing grapes or killing chickens."

New Data Supports Deterrence

Until now, believers in the deterrence effect of executions have had little hard evidence with which to counter such straw man debating techniques. The work of economist Isaac Ehrlich of the State University of New York in the 1970s, which found a significant deterrent effect, had been diluted by constant reinvestigation and criticism. In the end, it suffered most from being out of date, as it was based on evidence from before the suspension of the death penalty in 1972. Its relevance to the modern debate was therefore questionable.

But there now come impressive new findings from a trio of economists at Emory University in Georgia. Hashem Dezhbakhsh, Paul Rubin, and Joanna Mehlhop Shepherd released their paper "Does Capital Punishment Have a Deterrent Effect? New Evidence from Post-Moratorium Panel Data" in January 2001. Its findings are striking. The authors conclude that each execution deters other murders to the extent of saving between eight and twenty-eight innocent lives, with a best-estimate average of eighteen lives saved per execution.

The researchers reached this conclusion scientifically, by expressing the murder rate mathematically. They calculated the effect on the murder rate of a number of factors including, specifically, the likelihood of being arrested, the chance of being sentenced to death after arrest, and the chance of being executed after sentence. They were then able to work out how significant the chance of being executed is to the murder rate. They found that executions themselves are a very significant factor, certainly much more so than the simple removal of the murderer from the pool of potential killers. And their findings pass all the statistical tests that show that it's not just by chance that the math works that way. . . .

[I]t is important to look critically at the new work from Emory. The most obvious objection to the research is that it might fail to capture all the outside factors that feed the murder rate besides the criminal's rational assessment of his chances of getting caught. Factors such as drug trafficking, gun availability, and the overall supply of potentially violent young males are all recognized as important contributors to murder rates.

The researchers attempted to include these factors by constructing another element in their equation, taking account of crime rates for assault and robbery (which sometimes lead to murder), income levels, welfare levels, population density, six demographic categories for race and gender, and the state-level membership rate for the National Rifle Association (NRA), to serve as a proxy for gun ownership rates. They also took into account national-level trends such as the increasing amount of violence in America's popular culture. Finally, they added a variable to account for completely random factors. They then measured the results of their equations at both state and county levels, to give them as detailed a picture as possible. No earlier research, it is important to note, had ever gone into this level of detail.

Three Odd Results

Most of the results they obtained were as expected. The murder rate increased as assault and robbery increased, and it also varied with the number of males in a county and with the proportion of African-Americans. It decreased according to the size of the non-African-American minority population. It also decreased with higher population density, which may at first sight seem strange, but it should be borne in mind that rural areas, with low population density, often have higher murder rates than the peaceful suburbs.

Three results do, however, appear rather odd. The first is that the murder rate appears to increase with per capita income. The researchers explain this by suggesting that drug consumption, which is heavily linked to murder, may increase along with income. This is, however, speculation. The researchers did not include a true measure of drug consumption or trafficking in their equation, which is probably the biggest single mark against it. If, however, the researchers' assumption is true, it appears that the metropolitan elite's habit of purchasing drugs as a recreational luxury is contributing to the murder rate. This is not an argument that is often made in considering how the war against drugs should be fought, but it does provide food for thought.

Better Data Supports Deterrence Claims

Recent research on the relationship between capital punishment and crime has created a strong consensus among economists that capital punishment deters crime. Early studies from the 1970s and 1980s reached conflicting results. However, recent studies have exploited better data and more sophisticated statistical techniques. The modern studies have consistently shown that capital punishment has a strong deterrent effect, with each execution deterring between 3 and 18 murders. This is true even for crimes that might seem not to be deterrable, such as crimes of passion.

Joanna M. Shepherd, testimony before the House Judiciary Crime, Terrorism, and Homeland Security Subcommittee, April 24, 2004.

Another seemingly odd result is that a higher percentage of the population being teenage seems to lower the murder rate. This is again surprising, as the teen murder rate is the one that showed the biggest increase during the 1990s. It may be, however, that higher teenage populations involve proportionally more teenage girls, who are much less likely to murder than boys. Furthermore, the prime age for murder remains the immediate post-teen years, and it may be the size of *that* category that is most important. Unfortunately, the demographic category the researchers used was of ages twenty through twenty-nine, which includes large numbers who are putting their risky pasts behind them.

The final odd result was that the size of the state's NRA membership seems to increase the murder rate. This cannot be an effect of the murder rate rather than a cause, because the researchers took time lags into account in their models. NRA membership may, however, be a good indicator of the violence potential in a state, as states that have been previously more inclined to violence during earlier crime cycles retain high membership rates. States that have no real history of murder, however, may have fewer NRA members, as there is less need to join for self-protective purposes.

What the Study Implies

Despite all these reasonable explanations for the few odd results, the latter create enough doubt to cause one to worry about the robustness, if not the direction, of the authors' overall conclusion about deterrence. . . . Perhaps the best thing to happen to this research on capital punishment would be for the opponents of the death penalty to attack the assumptions and modeling techniques on which the findings rely. The researchers would then be forced to refine their model to rebut the attacks, by, for instance, including a measure of drug trafficking offenses or the like in the equation. If the conclusions still held true after such refinements, then the argument would be bolstered further.

In a way, this research is already a refinement and updating of Ehrlich's earlier work. It seeks, for instance, to answer the Cuomo argument that not all murders are rational, by estimating the number of murders that are unpreventable by deterrence and controlling for that factor. Similarly, the use of data collected since the restoration of the death penalty makes the research reasonably up-to-date. The use of county-level data avoids the problem that arises from using only national-level data, that of being unable to assess the true effects of individual states' policies. By any measure, this study is already a hugely important contribution to the debate.

[T]he implications are huge. By the study's estimate, the two recent federal executions will save approximately thirty-six lives. On the final day of 1999 (the last day for which we have accurate figures), there were 3,527 prisoners under sentence of death in American prisons. This study suggests that if all those sentences were carried out *63,000 lives* would be saved. There were approximately 15,000 homicides in America in 1999, meaning that the deterrence effect could be the equivalent of four years free from murder. Even the most committed opponents of the death penalty should take notice of that figure.

> "The value of [social science] research is
> shown by its success in demonstrating that
> capital punishment has not deterred
> homicide."

Studies Show That the Death Penalty Does Not Deter Crime

Ted Goertzel

Studies by economists claiming that the death penalty deters crime are faulty, contends Ted Goertzel in the following viewpoint. He argues that these researchers confirm their own biases by setting up mathematical models in such a way as to guarantee that research findings will support their position. Goertzel asserts that traditional comparative sociological research, which is far superior to this new econometric method, reveals that the death penalty has no deterrent effect. Goertzel is a professor of sociology at Rutgers University.

As you read, consider the following questions:

1. According to Goertzel, why does former attorney general Janet Reno's interpretation of the death penalty as a deterrent differ from Senator Orrin Hatch's interpretation?
2. Who conducted the first comparative study of capital punishment in the United States and what did he find out, as reported by the author?
3. What are Goertzel's chief criticisms of the econometric method when used in studying the death penalty?

Ted Goertzel, "Capital Punishment and Homicide: Sociological Realities and Econometric Illusions," *Skeptical Inquirer*, vol. 8, July/August 2004, pp. 23–28. Copyright © 2004 by the Committee for the Scientific Investigation of Claims of the Paranormal. Reproduced by permission.

I have inquired for most of my adult life about studies that might show that the death penalty is a deterrent, and I have not seen any research that would substantiate that point.

—Attorney General Janet Reno, January 20, 2000

All of the scientifically valid statistical studies—those that examine a period of years, and control for national trends—consistently show that capital punishment is a substantial deterrent.

—Senator Orrin Hatch, October 16, 2002

It happens all too often. Each side in a policy debate quotes studies that support its point of view and denigrates those from the other side. The result is often that research evidence is not taken seriously by either side. This has led some researchers, especially in the social sciences, to throw up their hands in dismay and give up studying controversial topics. But why bother doing social science research at all if it is impossible to obtain accurate and trustworthy information about issues that matter to people?

There are some questions that social scientists should be able to answer. Either executing people cuts the homicide rate or it does not. Or perhaps it does under certain conditions and not others. In any case, the data are readily available and researchers should be able to answer the question. Of course, this would not resolve the ethical issues surrounding the question, but that is another matter.

So who is right, Janet Reno or Orrin Hatch? And why can they not at least agree on what the data show? The problem is that each of them refers to bodies of research using different research methods. Janet Reno's statement correctly describes the results of studies that compare homicide trends in states and countries that practice capital punishment with those that do not. These studies consistently show that capital punishment has no effect on homicide rates. Orrin Hatch refers to studies that use econometric modeling. He is wrong, however, in stating that these studies *all* find that capital punishment deters homicide. In fact, some of them find a deterrent effect and some do not.

But this is not a matter of taste. It cannot be that capital punishment deters homicide for comparative researchers but not for econometricians. In fact, the comparative method has produced valid, useful, and consistent findings, while econometrics has failed in this and every similar area of research.

The Ground Rules for Capital Punishment Studies

The first of the comparative studies of capital punishment was done by Thorsten Sellin in 1959. Sellin was a sociologist at the University of Pennsylvania and one of the pioneers of scientific criminology. He was a prime mover in setting up the government agencies that collect statistics on crime. . . .

Sellin applied his combination of qualitative and quantitative methods in an exhaustive study of capital punishment in American states. He used every scrap of data that was available, together with his knowledge of the history, economy, and social structure of each state. He compared states to other states and examined changes in states over time. Every comparison he made led him to the "inevitable conclusion . . . that executions have no discernable effect on homicide rates."

Sellin's work has been replicated time and time again, as new data have become available, and all of the replications have confirmed his finding that capital punishment does not deter homicide. These studies are an outstanding example of what statistician David Freedman (1991) calls "shoe leather" social research. The hard work is collecting the best available data, both quantitative and qualitative. Once the statistical data are collected, the analysis consists largely in displaying them in tables, graphs, and charts which are then interpreted in light of qualitative knowledge of the states in question. This research can be understood by people with only modest statistical background. This allows consumers of the research to make their own interpretations, drawing on their qualitative knowledge of the states in question. . . .

Hundreds of comparisons of this sort have been made, and they consistently show that the death penalty has no effect. There have also been international comparative studies. [Researchers] examined fourteen countries that abolished the death penalty and found that abolition did not cause an increase in homicide rates. This research has been convincing to most criminologists which is why Janet Reno was told that there was no valid research linking capital punishment to homicide rates.

A Different Methodology

The studies that Orrin Hatch referred to use a very different methodology: econometrics, also known as multiple regression modeling, structural equation modeling, or path analysis. This involves constructing complex mathematical models on the assumption that the models mirror what happens in the real world. As I argued in a [2002] *Skeptical Inquirer* article, this method has consistently failed to offer reliable and valid results in studies of social problems where the data are very limited. Its most successful use is in making predictions in areas where there is a large flow of data for testing. The econometric literature on capital punishment has been carefully reviewed by several prominent economists and found wanting. There is simply too little data and too many ways to manipulate it. In one careful review, [economist Walter] McManus found that: "there is much uncertainty as to the 'correct' empirical model that should be used to draw inferences, and each researcher typically tries dozens, perhaps hundreds, of specifications before selecting one or a few to report. Usually, and understandably, the ones selected for publication are those that make the strongest case for the researcher's prior hypothesis."...

Since there are so many ways to model inadequate data, McManus was able to show that researchers whose prior beliefs led them to structure their models in different ways would obtain predictable conclusions: "The data analyzed are not sufficiently strong to lead researchers with different prior beliefs to reach a consensus regarding the deterrent effects of capital punishment. Right-winger, rational-maximizer, and eye-for-an-eye researchers will infer that punishment deters would-be murderers, but bleeding-heart and crime-of-passion researchers will infer that there is no significant deterrent effect."...

Unfortunately, econometricians continue to use multiple regression on capital punishment data and to generate results that are cited in Congressional hearings. In recent examples, [researchers in 2001] concluded that each execution decreases the number of homicides by five or six while [other researchers in 2002] argued that each execution deters eighteen murders. [Still another team in 2001] published a study finding that the Texas moratorium from March 1996 to April 1997 increased homicide rates, even though no increase can be seen. The moratorium simply increased homicide in comparison to what their econometric model said it would have otherwise been. Of all the econometric myths, the wildest is this: We know what would have been. . . .

Murder Rates in Death Penalty and Non–Death Penalty States*

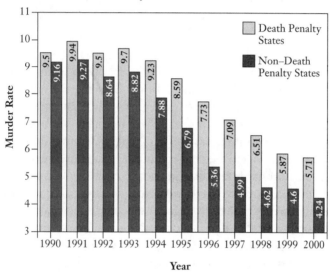

*Includes Kansas and New York, which adopted the death penalty in 1994 and 1995 respectively.

"Murder Rates in Death Penalty and Non–Death Penalty States," Death Penalty Information Center, 2004.

[Researchers] argue that when a large number of such studies give the same result, this provides "robust evidence" which "causes any neutral observer pause." But if McManus is correct that econometricians are likely to specify models to fit their preconceptions, then if many of them reach the same conclusion it may just mean that they have the same bias. Actually, there are a variety of biases among econometricians, which is why there are almost as many on one side as on the other of this issue. . . .

Mathematics vs. Good Social Science

Econometricians often dismiss the kind of comparative research that Thorsten Sellin did as crude and unsophisticated when compared to their use of complex mathematical formulas. But mathematical complexity does not make for good social science. The goal of multiple regression is to convert messy sociological realities into math problems that can be resolved with the certainty of mathematical proof. Econometricians believe they can control for the myriad variables that affect homicide rates, just as a chemist eliminates impurities to see how two chemicals interact in their pure form. . . .

It would be handy for social scientists if we lived in a [place] where everything else was equal and questions could be answered with a few calculations. But multivariate statistical analysis does not answer real-world questions such as, "does Texas, with a high execution rate, have a lower homicide rate than similar states?" or "did the homicide rate go down when Texas began executing people, compared to trends in other states that did not?" Instead, it answers the question, "If we use the latest, most sophisticated statistical methods to control for extraneous variables, can we say that the death penalty deters homicide rates *other things being equal?*" After decades of effort by many diligent researchers, we now know the answer to this question: There are many ways to adjust things statistically, and the answer will depend on which one is chosen. We also know that of the many possible ways to specify a regression model, each researcher is likely to prefer one that will give results consistent with his or her predispositions. . . .

Social science can provide valid and reliable results with methods that present the data with as little statistical manipulation as possible and interpret it in light of the best qualitative information available. The value of this research is shown by its success in demonstrating that capital punishment has not deterred homicide.

"Increasing the potential penalties for all crimes of terrorism will serve as a reminder to would-be terrorists that the murder of innocent Americans will be punished to the fullest extent allowed under our Constitution."

The Death Penalty Protects Americans from Terrorism

Johnny Sutton

In the following viewpoint, excerpted from congressional testimony on the Terrorist Penalties Enhancement Act of 2003 (House Resolution 2934), Johnny Sutton argues that the death penalty should be applied to terrorists to protect Americans from terrorist acts. He contends that the death penalty will be a powerful weapon in the war on terrorism when it is used to punish terrorists and remove them from society. The House of Representatives did not vote on HR 2934 and began hearings on the Terrorist Penalties Enhancement Act of 2005 in June 2005. Johnny Sutton is the attorney for the Western District of Texas.

As you read, consider the following questions:
1. What three purposes ought a weapon in the war on terrorism have, according to Sutton?
2. How does House Resolution 2934 enhance the USA PATRIOT Act in its treatment of terrorists?
3. What experience does Sutton cite as making him a good spokesperson in support of HR 2934?

Johnny Sutton, testimony before the U.S. House Subcommittee on Crime, Terrorism, and Homeland Security, Committee on the Judiciary, Washington, DC, April 21, 2004.

Thank you for the opportunity to appear before you to-day [April 21, 2004] to discuss H.R. [House Resolution] 2934, the "Terrorist Penalties Enhancement Act of 2003,"[1] and the importance of the death penalty in terrorism prosecutions.

The Death Penalty: An Important Weapon

In the war on terrorism, prosecutors must be equipped with every possible weapon that can help to prevent and deter terrorist conduct before it occurs, severely punish such conduct when it does occur, and help find justice for those whose lives have been affected by crimes of terror.

Following the [September 11, 2001, terrorist attacks], Congress wisely acted to improve and enhance federal law enforcement's terrorism fighting capabilities by overwhelmingly passing the USA PATRIOT Act. On a variety of fronts, the PATRIOT Act has provided tremendous tools for preventing terrorist acts and prosecuting terrorists. Among other things, the PATRIOT Act has effectively removed obstacles to crucial information-sharing between intelligence and law enforcement professionals, it has brought federal criminal law up-to-date with new technology, thus leveling the playing field for investigators and prosecutors, and it has increased the maximum sentences for a number of terrorism-related offenses. Despite these positive developments, more can and should be done, including the passage of H.R. 2934.

H.R. 2934 is important, because it will ensure that all terrorists who cause death in the course of their terroristic acts will be eligible for the death penalty if the facts warrant such a punishment. Under current law, some terrorist offenses that result in the death of American citizens do not provide for the death penalty or even for a sentence of life in prison as an available punishment. For example, a terrorist who is convicted of attacking a national defense installation, sabotaging a nuclear facility, or destroying a power plant cannot receive the death penalty, even if his crime results in mass casualties. As the President stated just two days ago, on April

1. HR 2934 was not brought to a vote in the House of Representatives. The Terrorist Penalties Enhancement Act of 2005 is under discussion in 2005.

19, 2004, this "makes no sense to me. We ought to be sending a strong signal: If you sabotage a defense installation or nuclear facility in a way that takes an innocent life, you ought to get the death penalty, the federal death penalty."

A Judge's Perspective

As a former State district judge for over 20 years, I have a unique perspective on the criminal system. I understand the importance of safety and the need for America to be tough on criminals. We must protect our neighborhoods from the threat of violent crimes which, unfortunately in today's world, includes the threat of terrorist attacks. Congress must act to protect U.S. citizens from such attacks and to bring justice to those who threaten our freedom.

It is unimaginable to think that a convicted terrorist responsible for American deaths could serve his sentence and be released back into the American streets free to act as he chooses. . . . In my experience as a Judge, I have witnessed the death penalty used as an important tool in deterring crime and saving lives. I believe it is a tool that can deter acts of terrorism. It protects witnesses in capital punishment cases, and it serves as a tool for prosecutors when negotiating sentences.

John R. Carter, statement before the Subcommittee on Crime, Terrorism, and Homeland Security, Judiciary Committee, House of Representatives, April 21, 2004.

H.R. 2934 would change the law to make the perpetrators of all terrorist acts resulting in death, including these, eligible for the death penalty. Increasing the potential penalties for all crimes of terrorism will serve as a reminder to would-be terrorists that the murder of innocent Americans will be punished to the fullest extent allowed under our Constitution.

A Serious and Sobering Business

As an experienced prosecutor at both the state and federal levels in my home state of Texas, I have had significant experience with death penalty cases. As a local prosecutor, I have personally tried three cases in which the death penalty was imposed, and considered a number of cases in which the State decided not to seek the death penalty. I have personally witnessed an execution, and understand the gravity of the ultimate punishment on both the perpetrator and victims of crime. During my tenure as the U.S. Attorney for the Western District of Texas, my office has considered 25 defendants charged with crimes eligible for the death penalty. My office has sought the death penalty in only one of those cases. In that case, the defendant was convicted, and the jury imposed the death penalty. Seeking and applying the death penalty is serious and sobering business. There is great responsibility in the exercise of prosecutorial discretion in this area. The Department of Justice has taken this responsibility seriously. Through its formal review process, the Department carefully reviews the applicability of the death penalty in every possible case, all the way up to the Attorney General. H.R. 2934 would not change this. I do not favor liberally expanding the number and types of crimes that may be punished by death. But in the fight against terrorism, we should have every tool at our disposal for dealing with those who commit or would commit such horrendous crimes of violence against our nation and our citizens. H.R. 2934 is an important contribution to that end. . . .

Again, thank you for inviting me to appear before your Subcommittee today. On behalf of the Department of Justice, I cannot thank you and your colleagues enough for the leadership and support you have provided in the war on terror. It is my pleasure to support H.R. 2934.

"The most dangerous terrorists do not fear death—they seek it."

The Death Penalty Makes Americans More Vulnerable to Terrorists

Timothy H. Edgar

The following viewpoint has been excerpted from congressional testimony on House Resolution 2934, the Terrorist Penalties Enhancement Act of 2003. In it Timothy H. Edgar argues against expanding the death penalty to include all terrorist acts. He claims that expanding the death penalty will make Americans less safe from terrorists for two essential reasons. First, the expansion, according to Edgar, would damage international cooperation that the United States needs to fight the war on terrorism. Most of America's allies, he points out, are opposed to the death penalty. Second, Edgar asserts that sentencing terrorists to death might actually encourage extremists who seek publicity for their causes. The bill was not acted upon by Congress in 2004. Timothy H. Edgar is the legislative counsel for the American Civil Liberties Union.

As you read, consider the following questions:

1. Under the proposed legislation discussed in this viewpoint, what crimes are being added as death penalty offenses?
2. How will the expansion of the death penalty affect the extradition of suspected terrorists from foreign countries, according to Edgar?
3. What is the "reverse deterrent effect" Edgar mentions?

Timothy H. Edgar, testimony before the U.S. House Subcommittee on Crime, Terrorism, and Homeland Security, Committee on the Judiciary, Washington, DC, April 21, 2004.

The proposed legislation[1] [Terrorist Penalties Enhancement Act of 2003] which expands the death penalty to acts defined by the USA PATRIOT Act as "terrorism" that are federal crimes punishable by more than one year in prison, is one part of a planned sequel to the USA PATRIOT Act commonly known as "Patriot Act 2." Congress should not consider such an expansion of the USA PATRIOT Act until it has undertaken comprehensive oversight of the federal government's use of the Act and its other law enforcement powers.

The bill's expansion of the federal death penalty would be drastic. In addition to creating twenty-three separate new death penalties in one stroke, the bill also creates an unprecedented "catch-all" death penalty for any federal crime, or any attempt or conspiracy to commit such a crime, that meets the PATRIOT Act's overbroad definition of terrorism and is punishable by more than one year in prison.

Such a drastic expansion of the death penalty will not make America safer from terrorism. Rather, it will undermine international cooperation against terrorism by further complicating efforts to obtain the cooperation of governments that have abolished the death penalty.

Adding even more death penalties will not deter suicidal, religiously motivated terrorists who have not been deterred by the twenty federal death penalties for crimes of terrorism already on the books (not to mention other federal and state death penalties that may be available) and may instead simply attract new followers to the cause. . . .

The radical expansion of the death penalty provided in [this legislation] would not aid in preventing terrorism or making America safer. Instead, the legislation is likely to significantly impede international cooperation in combating terrorism by creating new barriers to international legal assistance. Already, many nations that have abolished the death penalty are unwilling to extradite or provide evidence in federal terrorism cases if the death penalty might result from their cooperation.

---

1. A version of this legislation continues to be discussed in the House of Representatives as of July 1, 2005, as the Terrorist Penalties Enhancement Act of 2005.

The Death Penalty May Strengthen Terrorists

The natural demand for retribution after a terrorist organization has committed mass murder and other heinous crimes needs to be tempered by the fact that carrying out the death penalty may strengthen the terrorists. Given the perceived and actual grievances that the Arab and the greater Islamic worlds have towards the West in general and the United States in particular, carrying out such executions will probably tend to inflame the Arab and Islamic worlds, increase their support of terrorist movements and thwart cooperation with our allies, almost all of whom have abolished the death penalty. In addition, assuming the evidence at trial fails to show that Zacarias Moussaoui directly participated in the conspiracy to carry out the September 11 [2001, terrorist] attacks, executing him may be contrary to our current death penalty jurisprudence and would appear unjust to our allies and the Islamic world alike. Even if the evidence shows that Moussaoui directly participated in the September 11 conspiracy, executing him will . . . almost certainly make him the twentieth martyr for Muslims. . . .

We should . . . learn from the mistakes and the successes of Great Britain in fighting the IRA [Irish Republican Army], that executing politically motivated agents of terror is likely to spawn greater terrorism. Such restraint is a surer path towards isolating al Qaeda [terrorist group] and its allies in the lands of the aggrieved and the repressed. The death penalty is a luxury that we can ill afford in this international struggle.

Thomas Michael McDonnell, *Vanderbilt Journal of Transnational Law*, March 2004.

Other nations have become increasingly critical of the United States for its continued and even expanding use of the death penalty when the international trend has been towards abolition. The exoneration of more than one hundred former inmates of America's death row has not gone unnoticed abroad. Diplomacy concerning the issue of the death penalty has become increasingly tense and complex. The rift between the United States and many of its closest allies is likely to grow even wider as a result of a recent decision of the International Court of Justice concerning the death penalty. The decision strongly rebuked the United States for its disregard of the rights of 51 Mexican nationals on death row to timely consular notification under the Vienna Convention on Consular Relations.

The European Union prohibits the extradition of any criminal suspect facing the death penalty. After the bombing of United States embassies in Africa by Al Qaeda terrorists, Germany only extradited an alleged conspirator to face trial in the United States after negotiating assurances the suspect would not face the death penalty. Many European nations, including the United Kingdom, have restated their opposition to the death penalty after September 11, 2001 [terrorist attacks] and conditioned any extraditions in connection with the global fight against terrorism on similar assurances.

By dramatically expanding the number of death-eligible offenses, the bill would dramatically multiply the number of cases in which prosecutors will have to negotiate special agreements with foreign governments to obtain needed cooperation in obtaining evidence or extraditing suspects.

A dramatic expansion of the death penalty would, according to foreign policy experts, be likely to further impede the cooperation between nations that is absolutely critical to impeding terrorist organizations by arresting and prosecuting their members. Milt Bearden, a former CIA station chief in Pakistan and Sudan, warns, "If the U.S. routinely applies the death penalty to cases of international terrorism targeting American citizens, it may limit continued cooperation from the majority of countries most closely involved in combating terrorism."

Continuing and pronounced racial disparities in the imposition of the death sentence for serious street crimes has contributed to the harsh international criticism of the United States. A dramatic expansion of the death penalty for crimes said to be terror-related—making death-eligible many crimes that would not normally carry a death sentence—would confirm the suspicions of many in the Arab and Muslim world that the United States is creating a separate, and unequal, system of justice for mainly Arab and Muslim defendants.

Finally, the addition of new death penalty offenses to the federal government's already considerable arsenal of twenty death-eligible terrorism crimes will almost certainly have no deterrent effect on suicidal, religiously-motivated terrorists such as members of Al Qaeda. Well-publicized executions are far more likely to have a perverse "reverse deterrent effect." Terrorist groups will use the executions as propaganda to attract new followers who will be asked to emulate the "courage" of the "martyr."

The United States government should not go out of its way to provide terrorists with the gift of publicity—often the most important tactical goal of any terrorist action. Jessica Stern, a terrorism expert and former member of the National Security Council, warns that executions of terrorists can "turn criminals into martyrs, invite retaliatory strikes, and enhance the public relations and fund-raising strategies of our enemies."

Put simply, the most dangerous terrorists do not fear death —they seek it. Even for those who do not participate in suicide attacks, the risks inherent in terrorist activity are far more significant than the possibility that a death sentence would be imposed on any given terrorist suspect.

While some may argue the death penalty can be used to obtain cooperation of suspects, other countries with more experience in countering terrorist organizations have specifically rejected the death penalty for terrorists. While imprisoning terrorists also carries risks, these nations have determined that the risks of executions are greater, outweighing any potential benefits. For example, the United Kingdom voted to repeal the death penalty for terrorism in Northern Ireland on the basis that executing terrorists only increases violence and puts soldiers and police at greater risk.

Spain similarly rejected the death penalty as counterproductive in its decades-long campaign against the Basque terrorist group ETA. Even as the Israeli government continues its controversial tactic of targeted killings of terrorist suspects, its judges do not impose the death penalty on terrorists in Israeli custody. . . .

H.R. 2934 will rightly be seen, both in the United States and abroad, as another federal infringement on civil liberties that will not make America safer. It will, as a result, increase mistrust, both at home and abroad, even of legitimate anti-terrorism efforts, dividing many Americans from their government and further isolating America in the world. It should be rejected.

Periodical Bibliography

The following articles have been selected to supplement the diverse views presented in this chapter.

Amnesty International   "The Death Penalty Is Not a Deterrent," 2002. www.amnestyusa.org.

Joseph Carroll   "Americans and the Death Penalty," *Gallup Poll News Service*, December 15, 2004.

Cavalier Daily   "Death to the Death Penalty," September 24, 2004. www.cavalierdaily.com.

Douglas Clement   "A Punishing Debate: Does the Death Penalty Deter Homicide? New Economic Studies Seek the Answer to an Age-Old Question," *Region*, June 2002. www.minneapolisfed.org.

James M. Galliher   "A 'Commonsense' Theory of Deterrence and the 'Ideology' of Science: The New York State Death Penalty Debate," *Journal of Criminal Law and Criminology*, Fall 2001/Winter 2002.

R.J. Gerber   "Economic and Historical Implications for Capital Punishment Deterrence," *Notre Dame Journal of Law, Ethics, and Public Policy*, 2004.

Allan D. Johnson   "The Illusory Death Penalty: Why America's Death Penalty Process Fails to Support the Economic Theories of Criminal Sanctions and Deterrence," *Hastings Law Journal*, July 2001.

Helmut Kury   "Does Severe Punishment Mean Less Criminality?" *International Criminal Justice Review*, 2003.

H. Naci Mocan and R. Kaj Gittings   "Getting Off Death Rows: Commuted Sentences and the Deterrent Effect of Capital Punishment," *Journal of Law and Economics*, October 2003.

John O'Sullivan   "A Logical and Just Practice," *National Review*, July 17, 2000.

Michael L. Radelet   "The Changing Nature of Death Penalty Debates," *Annual Review of Sociology*, 2000.

Maimon Schwarzschild   "Retribution, Deterrence, and the Death Penalty: A Response to Hugo Bedau," *Criminal Justice Ethics*, Summer/Fall 2002.

Jessica Stern   "Execute Terrorists at Our Own Risk," *New York Times*, February 28, 2001.

Cass R. Sunstein and Adrian Vermeule   "Is Capital Punishment Morally Required?: The Relevance of Life-Life Tradeoffs," Working Paper 05-06, AEI-Brookings Joint Center for Regulatory Studies, March 2005. www.aei-brookings.org.

CHAPTER 3

Is the Death Penalty Applied Fairly?

Chapter Preface

The issue of fair application of the death penalty is one that surfaces in many debates. Fairness implies that any person charged with a capital crime, regardless of race, religion, socioeconomic status, national origin, or geographic location, will receive the same treatment under the law than any other person charged with the same crime. In addition, fairness also requires that the death penalty (the most severe punishment applied in the United States) be reserved for the criminal who commits the most terrible crime. While establishing fairness might seem to be reasonable and straightforward, many factors complicate the task.

Critics of the death penalty point to studies that indicate racial discrimination in death penalty sentencing. James S. Liebman, a Columbia Law School professor, asserts in a 2002 report that errors in death penalty cases occur much more frequently in states with higher proportions of African Americans than in states with fewer African Americans. Those who advocate the death penalty, however, insist that it is a misreading of statistics to charge racial bias in death penalty sentencing. They contend that more blacks are sentenced because more blacks than whites commit capital crimes.

Juvenile capital punishment is another important issue in the debate. During the last decades of the twentieth century, most states enacted laws that made it easier to try juveniles as adults, making them eligible for the death penalty in some states. Such changes in law reflected public opinion: A 2000 Gallup poll reported that 65 percent of Americans thought juveniles should be treated as adults in the criminal justice system. However, in March 2005 the Supreme Court ruled that juveniles could no longer be subject to the death penalty, regardless of individual state law. Death penalty opponents cite studies in adolescent brain development suggesting that juveniles are not fully culpable for their crimes. Death penalty advocates assert that punishment should fit the crime regardless of the age of the offender.

DNA technology also adds a new dimension to the fairness debate. DNA testing can establish the presence of an individual at the scene of a crime, thus reducing potential error. Many death row exonerations have been the result of postconviction DNA testing. The Justice for All Act, passed in 2004, provides for the increased use of DNA evidence in capital trials. However, critics of the death penalty point out that defendants many not have fair access to DNA technology due to case overload at crime labs.

A final issue of fairness is that of defense attorney competence. All defendants are guaranteed representation at trial by the Constitution; however, critics of the death penalty point out that many court-appointed attorneys do not have the expertise they need to prepare an adequate defense in complicated capital cases. As Michael Radelet writes in his book *The Death Penalty in America: Twenty-five Years After* Gregg v. Georgia, "Whether one lives or dies seems more a function of the defendant's legal counsel or pure luck than any of the relevant characteristics of the crime or the offender's prior record." Prosecutors and state's attorneys general, while agreeing that defense attorneys must meet minimum competency guidelines, argue that defendants are well represented by their court-appointed attorneys. They point to many legal reforms such as the 2004 Justice for All Act, which mandates standards for defense attorneys in death penalty trials.

The writers of the viewpoints in this chapter investigate the issue of fairness. They examine race, the implications of DNA testing, human error, and attorney expertise.

"Race severely disadvantages the black jurors, black defendants, and black victims."

The Death Penalty Discriminates Against Racial Minorities

Christina Swarns

In the following viewpoint Christina Swarns argues that chief prosecutors (who are overwhelmingly white) have unfettered discretion in choosing which cases will be death penalty cases. Swarns asserts that prosecutors use this discretion to select more black than white defendants for death penalty cases. Further, more murderers of white victims face the death penalty than do murderers of black victims. Prosecutors also exclude potential jurors who are black from capital cases, according to Swarns. Christina Swarns is director of the National Association for the Advancement of Colored People Legal Defense Fund's Criminal Justice Project.

As you read, consider the following questions:

1. What is "prosecutorial discretion"?
2. What proof does Swarns offer that prosecutors "exercise their discretion along racial lines"?
3. How does the racial makeup of a jury in a capital case affect the sentencing of defendants?

Christina Swarns, "The Uneven Scales of Capital Justice," *The American Prospect*, vol. 15, July 2004, pp. 14–16. Copyright © 2004 by The American Prospect, Inc. All rights reserved. Reproduced with permission of the author.

In 1972, the U.S. Supreme Court declared the death penalty unconstitutional. The Court found that because the capital-punishment laws gave sentencers virtually unbridled discretion in deciding whether or not to impose a death sentence, "The death sentence [was] disproportionately carried out on the poor, the Negro, and the members of unpopular groups."

In 1976, the Court reviewed the revised death-penalty statutes—which are in place today—and concluded that they sufficiently restricted sentencer discretion such that race and class would no longer play a pivotal role in the life-or-death calculus. In the 28 years since the reinstatement of the death penalty, however, it has become apparent that the Court was wrong. Race and class remain critical factors in the decision of who lives and who dies.

Both race and poverty corrupt the administration of the death penalty. Race severely disadvantages the black jurors, black defendants, and black victims within the capital-punishment system. Black defendants are more likely to be executed than white defendants. Those who commit crimes against black victims are punished less severely than those who commit crimes against white victims. And black potential jurors are often denied the opportunity to serve on death-penalty juries. As far as the death penalty is concerned, therefore, blackness is a proxy for worthlessness.

Poverty is a similar—and often additional—handicap. Because the lawyers provided to indigent defendants charged with capital crimes are so uniformly undertrained and undercompensated, the 90 percent of capitally charged defendants who lack the resources to retain a private attorney are virtually guaranteed a death sentence. Together, therefore, race and class function as an elephant on death's side of the sentencing scale.

How Race Affects the Death Penalty

When and how does race infect the death-penalty system? The fundamental lesson of the Supreme Court's 1972 decision to strike down the death penalty is that discretion, if left unchecked, will be exercised in such a manner that arbitrary and irrelevant factors like race will enter into the sentencing decision. That conclusion remains true today. The points at which discretion is exercised are the gateways through which racial bias continues to enter into the sentencing calculation.

Blind Justice?

Nearly 120 years ago, Frederick Douglass, the former slave and great African American leader, described the American criminal justice system as follows: "Justice is often painted with bandaged eyes. She is described in forensic eloquence, as utterly blind to wealth or poverty, high or low, white or black, but a mask of iron, however thick, could never blind American justice, when a black man happens to be on trial." Sadly, little has changed in the century and a half since Douglass had cause to condemn the state of the justice system in America. Nowhere is this more true than in the application of the "ultimate punishment"—the punishment of death.

Charles J. Ogletree, *Oregon Law Review*, Spring 2002.

Who has the most unfettered discretion? Chief prosecutors, who are overwhelmingly white, make some of the most critical decisions vis-à-vis the death penalty. Because their decisions go unchecked, prosecutors have arguably the greatest unilateral influence over the administration of the death penalty.

Prosecutorial Discretion

Do prosecutors exercise their discretion along racial lines? Unquestionably yes. Prosecutors bring more defendants of color into the death-penalty system than they do white defendants. For example, a 2000 study by the U.S. Department of Justice reveals that between 1995 and 2000, 72 percent of the cases that the attorney general approved for death-penalty prosecution involved defendants of color. During that time, statistics show that there were relatively equal numbers of black and white homicide perpetrators.

Prosecutors also give more white defendants than black defendants the chance to avoid a death sentence. Specifically, prosecutors enter into plea bargains—deals that allow capitally charged defendants to receive a lesser sentence in exchange for an admission of guilt—with white defendants far more often than they do with defendants of color. Indeed, the Justice Department study found that white defendants were almost twice as likely as black defendants to enter into such plea agreements.

Further, prosecutors assess cases differently depending upon the race of the victim. Thus, the Department of Justice found that between 1995 and 2000, U.S. attorneys were almost twice as likely to seek the death penalty for black defendants accused of killing nonblack victims than for black defendants accused of killing black victims.

Prosecutors Exclude Black Jurors

And, finally, prosecutors regularly exclude black potential jurors from service in capital cases. For example, a 2003 study of jury selection in Philadelphia capital cases, conducted by the Pennsylvania Supreme Court Commission on Race and Gender Bias in the Justice System, revealed that prosecutors used peremptory challenges—the power to exclude potential jurors for any reason aside from race or gender—to remove 51 percent of black potential jurors while excluding only 26 percent of nonblack potential jurors. Such bias has a long history: From 1963 to 1976, one Texas prosecutor's office instructed its lawyers to exclude all people of color from service on juries by distributing a memo containing the following language: "Do not take Jews, Negroes, Dagos, Mexicans or a member of any minority race on a jury, no matter how rich or how well educated." This extraordinary exercise of discretion harms black capital defendants because statistics reveal that juries containing few or no blacks are more likely to sentence black defendants to death.

Such blatant prosecutorial discretion has significantly contributed to the creation of a system that is visibly permeated with racial bias. Black defendants are sentenced to death and executed at disproportionate rates. For example, in Philadelphia, African American defendants are approximately four times more likely to be sentenced to death than similarly situated white defendants. And nationwide, crimes against white victims are punished more severely than crimes against black victims. Thus, although 46.7 percent of all homicide victims are black, only 13.9 percent of the victims of executed defendants are black. In some jurisdictions, all of the defendants on death row have white victims; in other jurisdictions, having a white victim exponentially increases a criminal defendant's likelihood of being sentenced to death. It is beyond dispute, therefore, that race remains a central factor in the administration of the death penalty.

"Scholars have known for quite some time that capital punishment is not applied in a racist manner."

The Death Penalty Does Not Discriminate Against Racial Minorities

John Perazzo

Research does not support the notion that racial bias affects the application of the death penalty, argues John Perazzo in the following viewpoint. Statistics show that there is actually a disproportionately low execution rate for black murderers in light of the relatively high numbers of black prisoners serving murder sentences, Perazzo explains. In light of this information, he concludes, hurling charges of racism against the U.S. criminal justice system is irresponsible and unfair. Perazzo is the author of *The Myths That Divide Us: How Lies Have Poisoned American Race Relations.*

As you read, consider the following questions:

1. Which governor has recently expressed concerns about racial bias in the justice system, according to Perazzo?
2. According to the author, what percentage of whites arrested for murder are likely to be executed? What percentage of blacks?
3. What percentage of inmates on death row are black, according to Perazzo?

John Perazzo, "Does the Death Penalty Discriminate?" www.frontpagemag.com, June 5, 2002. Copyright © 2002 by the Center for the Study of Popular Culture. Reproduced by permission.

M aryland Governor Parris Glendening recently joined an ever-growing list of public officials and social activists to question the manner in which the death penalty is administered to convicted murderers in the US. Upon learning that nine of Maryland's thirteen current death-row inmates are black, Glendening expressed his concern about possible racial bias in the justice system and promptly suspended executions in his state.

Mr. Glendening has plenty of company in holding this position. The NAACP [National Association for the Advancement of Colored People] Legal Defense and Education Fund, for instance, asserts that "history and current practice continue to show that the death penalty is steeped in a tradition of racism and cannot, for that reason, be applied in a fair manner." According to Amnesty International, "The United States legal system is riddled with deeply ingrained racial and ethnic divisions. The prejudices of some police, jurors, judges and prosecutors reflect contemporary racial and ethnic divisions in US society and nowhere is racial discrimination more evident, or more deadly, than in the application of the death penalty." The National Coalition to Abolish the Death Penalty which is comprised of the American Civil Liberties Union, the National Urban League, and some 140 other organizations complains that capital punishment is overwhelmingly reserved for racial minorities. Representative John Conyers emphatically agrees.

Louis Farrakhan goes even further, stating that "the unfair use of the death penalty to punish the black male is in fact a systematic genocidal tool being institutionalized to significantly decrease the black population." In 1996, Rev. Jesse Jackson co-authored the book *Legal Lynching: Racism, Injustice, and the Death Penalty*. At a recent Chicago rally, Jackson compared the inherent racism underlying capital punishment to the inherent racism that once supported the institution of slavery. "You couldn't really fix slavery," said Jackson. "You couldn't modify it. . . . We had to abolish the slavery system. Let's abolish the death penalty."

If all the aforementioned charges were true, there would indeed be good reason to consider outlawing capital punishment. Certainly we cannot tolerate separate standards of justice based on race. Remarkably, however, none of the charges are true. While there may be valid moral and ethical reasons to oppose the death penalty, racial inequity is simply not one of them.

Prisoners on Death Row by Race, 2003

Race	Number of Death Row Inmates	Percentage of Death Row Inmates (Rounded to the nearest percent)
White	1878	56%
Black	1418	42%
American Indian	29	1%
Asian	35	1%
Unknown	14	<1%
Total	3374	100%

Capital Punishment Statistics, Bureau of Justice Statistics, January 13, 2005. www.ojp.usdoj.gov/bjs/cp.htm.

Consider the pertinent facts. According to the Bureau of Justice Statistics, whites who are arrested for murder or non-negligent manslaughter are actually more likely than their black counterparts to be sentenced to death (1.6 percent vs. 1.2 percent). Of those inmates under death sentences, whites are actually likelier than blacks to have their sentences carried out (7.2 percent vs. 5.9 percent). These disparities are not huge, and the purpose here is not to suggest that they indicate bias against whites; the point is that in no way do they support the notion of bias against blacks.

Contrary to the rhetoric of our contemporary racial arsonists and "civil rights" organizations, scholars have known for quite some time that capital punishment is not applied in a racist manner. In his 1987 book *The Myth of a Racist Criminal Justice System*, Professor William Wilbanks cites an important study which found that between 1977 and 1984, white killers were actually more likely to get the death penalty than were black killers. Even more to the point, Wilbanks notes that "whites who had killed whites were more likely than blacks who had killed whites to be on death row, [and] whites who killed blacks were more likely to reach death row than blacks who killed blacks." In other words, even a full generation ago the anti–capital punishment crowd's most popular contention was already nothing more than a hollow fable.

Race Plays No Significant Role

More recently, in their 1997 book *America in Black and White*, Stephan and Abigail Thernstrom point out that "black offenders over the past generation have not been sentenced to death at a higher rate than white offenders. No careful scholarly study in recent years has demonstrated that the race of the defendant has played a significant role in the outcome of murder trials." The Thernstroms also note that while fully 58 percent of prisoners currently serving sentences for murder are black, only 40 percent of inmates on death row are black. That is, relative to the rate at which black offenders commit murder, they are sentenced to death in disproportionately low numbers.

Finally, if courts were unfairly imposing the death penalty against black defendants who deserved more leniency, we would expect to find that blacks on death row have cleaner criminal records than their white counterparts. But in fact, the exact opposite is true. Blacks awaiting execution are 10 percent likelier to have had felony convictions, and 20 percent likelier to have had homicide convictions, prior to the crimes that propelled them to death row.

Is it possible that Governor Glendening is unaware of these thorny but vital facts? If so, is it not irresponsible of him to parade the haunting, oft-unfurled banner of racism before the eyes of the American people once again? Haven't our perceptions of reality already been compromised enough by the nonsense of demagogues in recent decades?

*"When a juvenile commits a heinous crime,
. . . the State cannot extinguish his life
and his potential to attain a mature
understanding of his own humanity."*

Juveniles Should Not Receive the Death Penalty

Anthony M. Kennedy

The following viewpoint summarizes the 2005 majority opinion of the U.S. Supreme Court concerning the death penalty for juveniles. According to Anthony M. Kennedy, "evolving standards of decency" have led the majority of Americans to view juvenile execution as cruel and unusual punishment. In addition, the Court held that like mentally incapacitated people (already protected from execution by a case decided in 2002), juveniles cannot be held fully responsible for their actions. Finally, Kennedy argues that international opinion confirms that the United States ought to prohibit juvenile executions. Associate Justice Kennedy was nominated for the Supreme Court by President Ronald Reagan, and he took his seat on the bench on February 18, 1988.

As you read, consider the following questions:

1. According to Kennedy, what are the circumstances of Christopher Simmons's case?
2. How does this case compare to the *Atkins v. Virginia* case, as related by Kennedy?
3. What general differences between adult and juvenile offenders does Kennedy cite as reasons for the Court's decision?

Anthony M. Kennedy, syllabus, *Roper v. Simmons*, 543 U.S., March 1, 2005.

At age 17, respondent [Christopher] Simmons planned and committed a capital murder. After he had turned 18, he was sentenced to death. His direct appeal and subsequent petitions for state and federal postconviction relief were rejected. This Court then held, in *Atkins v. Virginia*, [2002] the Eighth Amendment, applicable to the States through the Fourteenth Amendment, prohibits the execution of a mentally retarded person. Simmons filed a new petition for state postconviction relief, arguing that *Atkins'* reasoning established that the Constitution prohibits the execution of a juvenile who was under 18 when he committed his crime. The Missouri Supreme Court agreed and set aside Simmons' death sentence in favor of life imprisonment without eligibility for release. It held that, although *Stanford v. Kentucky* [1989], rejected the proposition that the Constitution bar capital punishment for juvenile offenders younger than 18, a national consensus has developed against the execution of those offenders since *Stanford*. . . .

The Court's Holding

The Eighth and Fourteenth Amendments forbid imposition of the death penalty on offenders who were under the age of 18 when their crimes were committed.

The Eighth Amendment's prohibition against "cruel and unusual punishments" must be interpreted according to its text, by considering history, tradition, and precedent, and with due regard for its purpose and function in the constitutional design. To implement this framework this Court has established the propriety and affirmed the necessity of referring to "the evolving standards of decency that mark the progress of a maturing society" to determine which punishments are so disproportionate as to be "cruel and unusual." In 1988, . . . a plurality determined that national standards of decency did not permit the execution of any offender under age 16 at the time of the crime. The next year, in *Stanford*, a 5-to-4 Court referred to contemporary standards of decency, but concluded the Eighth and Fourteenth Amendments did not proscribe the execution of offenders over 15 but under 18 because 22 of 37 death penalty States permitted that penalty for 16-year-old offenders, and 25 permitted it for 17-year-olds,

Wilkinson. © 1999 by the *Philadelphia Daily News*. Reproduced by permission of Signe Wilkinson & Writers Syndicate/cartoonweb.com.

thereby indicating there was no national consensus. A plurality also "emphatically reject[ed]" the suggestion that the Court should bring its own judgment to bear on the acceptability of the juvenile death penalty. That same day the Court held, in *Penry v. Lynaugh*, that the Eighth Amendment did not mandate a categorical exemption from the death penalty for mentally retarded persons because only two States had enacted laws banning such executions. Three terms ago in *Atkins*, however, the Court held that standards of decency had evolved since [1988] . . . and now demonstrated that the execution of the mentally retarded is cruel and unusual punishment. The *Atkins* Court noted that objective indicia [indications] of society's standards, as expressed in pertinent legislative enactments and state practice, demonstrated that such executions had become so truly unusual that it was fair to say that a national consensus has developed against them. The Court also returned to the rule, established in decisions predating *Stanford*, that the Constitution contemplates that the Court's own judgment be brought to bear on the question of the acceptability of the death penalty. After observing that mental retardation diminishes personal culpability even if the offender can distinguish right from wrong, and that mentally retarded offenders' impairments make it less defensible to impose the death penalty as retribution for past crimes or as a real deterrent to future crimes, the Court ruled that the death penalty constitutes an excessive sanction for the entire category of mentally retarded offenders, and that the Eighth Amendment places a substantive restriction on the State's power to take such an offender's life. Just as the *Atkins* Court reconsidered the issue decided in *Penry*, the Court now reconsiders the issue decided in *Stanford*.

From the Mentally Retarded to Juveniles

Both objective indicia of consensus, as expressed in particular by the enactments of legislatures that have addressed the question, and the Court's own determination in the exercise of its independent judgment, demonstrate that the death penalty is a disproportionate punishment for juveniles.

As in *Atkins*, the objective indicia of national consensus here—the rejection of the juvenile death penalty in the majority of States; the infrequency of its use even where it remains on the books; and the consistency in the trend toward abolition of the practice—provide sufficient evidence that today society views juveniles, in the words *Atkins* used respecting the mentally retarded, as "categorically less culpable than the average criminal." The evidence of such consensus is similar, and in some respects parallel, to the evidence in *Atkins*: 30 States prohibit the juvenile death penalty, including 12 that have rejected it altogether and 18 that maintain it but, by express provision or judicial interpretation, exclude juveniles from its reach. Moreover, even in the 20 States without a formal prohibition, the execution of juveniles is infrequent. Although, by contrast to *Atkins*, the rate of change in reducing the incidence of the juvenile death penalty, or in taking specific steps to abolish it, has been less dramatic, the difference between this case and *Atkins* in that respect is counterbalanced by the consistent direction of the change toward abolition. Indeed, the slower pace here may be explained by the simple fact that the impropriety of executing juveniles between 16 and 18 years old gained wide recognition earlier than the impropriety of executing the mentally retarded.

Rejection of the imposition of the death penalty on juve-

A Shameful Practice

Regardless of the documented horrors of any specific case, the juvenile death penalty is a "shameful practice," to use the words of Supreme Court Justices John Paul Stevens, David Souter, Ruth Bader Ginsburg and Stephen Breyer. The United States is now the only country that continues to execute juveniles. (The Democratic Republic of the Congo did it last in 2000; Iran in 2001.) And, despite all our showy commitment to extending human rights around the world, the United States is now the only country that has failed to ratify the United Nations Convention on the Rights of the Child, which includes a provision that prohibits capital punishment for those under the age of 18. What a curious position for a country whose President [George W. Bush] proclaims himself a compassionate conservative, declaring that "no child should be left behind." And what a disturbing contradiction for an Administration filled to the brim with Christian moralists, people who are supposed to demonstrate, in word as well as deed, a faith in the idea of redemption and the human capacity for change. As a historian who has studied juvenile death-penalty cases as far back as the nineteenth century, it's clear to me that these cases tend to become political footballs, used to attract votes by demonstrating the state's ability to deliver "disinterested" justice.

Joan Jacobs Brumberg, *The Nation*, November 17, 2003.

nile offenders under 18 is required by the Eighth Amendment. Capital punishment must be limited to those offenders who commit "a narrow category of the most serious crimes" and whose extreme culpability makes them "the most deserving of execution." Three general differences between juveniles under 18 and adults demonstrate that juvenile offenders cannot with reliability be classified among the worst offenders. Juveniles' susceptibility to immature and irresponsible behavior means "their irresponsible conduct is not as morally reprehensible as that of an adult." Their own vulnerability and comparative lack of control over their immediate surroundings mean juveniles have a greater claim than adults to be forgiven for failing to escape negative influences in their whole environment. The reality that juveniles still struggle to define their identity means it is less supportable to conclude that even a heinous crime committed by a juvenile is evidence of irretrievably depraved character. The *Thompson* plurality recognized the import of these characteristics with respect to juveniles under 16. The same reasoning applies to all juvenile offenders under 18. Once juveniles' diminished culpability is recognized, it is evident that neither of the two penological justifications for the death penalty—retribution and deterrence of capital crimes by prospective offenders provides adequate justification for imposing that penalty on juveniles. Although the Court cannot deny or overlook the brutal crimes too many juvenile offenders have committed, it disagrees with petitioner's contention that, given the Court's own insistence on individualized consideration in capital sentencing, it is arbitrary and unnecessary to adopt a categorical rule barring imposition of the death penalty on an offender under 18. An unacceptable likelihood exists that the brutality or cold-blooded nature of any particular crime would overpower mitigating arguments based on youth as a matter of course, even where the juvenile offender's objective immaturity, vulnerability, and lack of true depravity should require a sentence less severe than death. When a juvenile commits a heinous crime, the State can exact forfeiture of some of the most basic liberties, but the State cannot extinguish his life and his potential to attain a mature understanding of his own humanity. While drawing the line at 18 is subject to the objections always raised against categorical rules, that is the point where society draws the line for many purposes between childhood and adulthood and the age at which the line for death eligibility ought to rest. . . .

International Opinion

The overwhelming weight of international opinion against the juvenile death penalty is not controlling here, but provides respected and significant confirmation for the Court's determination that the penalty is disproportionate punishment for offenders under 18. The United States is the only country in the world that continues to give official sanction to the juvenile penalty. It does not lessen fidelity to the Constitution or pride in its origins to acknowledge that the express affirmation of certain fundamental rights by other nations and peoples underscores the centrality of those same rights within our own heritage of freedom.

4

"An especially depraved juvenile offender may . . . be just as culpable as many adult offenders considered bad enough to deserve the death penalty."

Juveniles Should Not Be Exempt from the Death Penalty

Sandra Day O'Connor

The following viewpoint is excerpted from Justice Sandra Day O'Connor's dissenting opinion on the U.S. Supreme Court's 2005 ruling prohibiting the death penalty for juveniles. She argues that there is insufficient evidence of a national consensus on the question of whether juvenile murderers should be put to death. Consequently, she maintains, the Court cannot appeal to the public's general censure of the juvenile death penalty to make its decision to prohibit the practice. Second, she asserts that juvenile offenders can be as culpable as adults when they commit particularly heinous crimes. Therefore, juveniles ought not be excluded as a class from the death penalty. Associate Justice O'Connor was nominated by President Ronald Reagan. She took her seat on the bench on September 25, 1981. O'Connor retired in July 2005.

As you read, consider the following questions:
1. What does O'Connor demand before she would be willing to categorically forbid the death penalty for juveniles?
2. How does O'Connor respond to the Court's three distinctions between adult and juvenile offenders?
3. What does O'Connor say she would do if she were a legislator rather than a judge?

Sandra Day O'Connor, dissenting opinion, *Roper v. Simmons*, 543 U.S., March 1, 2005.

The Court's decision today [March 1, 2005] establishes a categorical rule forbidding the execution of any offender for any crime committed before his 18th birthday, no matter how deliberate, wanton, or cruel the offense. Neither the objective evidence of contemporary societal values, nor the Court's moral proportionality analysis, nor the two in tandem suffice to justify this ruling.

Although the Court finds support for its decision in the fact that a majority of the States now disallow capital punishment of 17-year-old offenders, it refrains from asserting that its holding is compelled by a genuine national consensus. Indeed, the evidence before us fails to demonstrate conclusively that any such consensus has emerged in the brief period since we upheld the constitutionality of this practice in [1989].

Some Juveniles Deserve Death

Instead, the rule decreed by the Court rests, ultimately, on its independent moral judgment that death is a disproportionately severe punishment for any 17-year-old offender. I do not subscribe to this judgment. Adolescents *as a class* are undoubtedly less mature, and therefore less culpable for their misconduct, than adults. But the Court has adduced no evidence impeaching the seemingly reasonable conclusion reached by many state legislatures: that at least *some* 17-year-old murderers are sufficiently mature to deserve the death penalty in an appropriate case. Nor has it been shown that capital sentencing juries are incapable of accurately assessing a youthful defendant's maturity or of giving due weight to the mitigating characteristics associated with youth.

On this record . . . I would not substitute our judgment about the moral propriety of capital punishment for 17-year-old murderers for the judgments of the Nation's legislatures. Rather, I would demand a clearer showing that our society truly has set its face against this practice before reading the Eighth Amendment categorically to forbid it. . . .

The National Consensus

Here . . . the objective evidence of a national consensus is weaker than in most prior cases in which the Court has struck down a particular punishment under the Eighth Amendment. In my view, the objective evidence of national consensus, standing alone, was insufficient to dictate the Court's holding in *Atkins* [a 2002 case protecting mentally incapacitated people from the death penalty]. Rather, the compelling moral proportionality argument against capital punishment of mentally retarded offenders played a *decisive* role in persuading the Court that the practice was inconsistent with the Eighth Amendment. Indeed, the force of the proportionality argument in *Atkins* significantly bolstered the Court's confidence that the objective evidence in that case did, in fact, herald the emergence of a genuine national consensus. Here, by contrast, the proportionality argument against the juvenile death penalty is so flawed that it can be given little, if any, analytical weight—it proves too weak to resolve the lingering ambiguities in the objective evidence of legislative consensus or to justify the Court's categorical rule.

Juveniles and Adults

Seventeen-year-old murderers must be categorically exempted from capital punishment, the Court says, because they "cannot with reliability be classified among the worst offenders." That conclusion is premised on three perceived differences between "adults," who have already reached their 18th birthdays, and "juveniles," who have not. First, juveniles lack maturity and responsibility and are more reckless than adults. Second, juveniles are more vulnerable to outside influences because they have less control over their surroundings. And third, a juvenile's character is not as fully formed as that of an adult. Based on these characteristics, the Court determines that 17-year-old capital murderers are not as blameworthy as adults guilty of similar crimes; that 17-year-olds are less likely than adults to be deterred by the prospect of a death sentence; and that it is difficult to conclude that a 17-year-old who commits even the most heinous of crimes is "irretrievably depraved." The Court suggests that "a rare case might arise in which a juvenile offender has sufficient psychological maturity, and at the same time demonstrates sufficient depravity, to merit a sentence of death." However, the Court argues that a categorical age-based prohibition is justified as a prophylactic rule because "[t]he differences between juvenile and adult offenders are too marked and well understood to risk allowing a youthful person to receive the death penalty despite insufficient culpability."

Fully Culpable Killers

The vast majority of 16- and 17-year-olds know how wrong it is to kill another human being. They are fully capable of developing intelligent and frightful schemes for getting even with people who have made them angry. They can control themselves, even in the face of injustice or cruelty, and reject the option of responding with horrible violence. Also, the vast majority of 16- and 17-year-olds are as articulate, able to reason, and persuasive as they will ever be as adults. . . .

My primary concern is that capital punishment remain an option when a cold-blooded 16-year-old carries out a grisly gang-ordered murder. . . . He should not be able to kill secure in the knowledge that he is shielded from the ultimate punishment simply because he is some number of days away from his 18th birthday.

Jerry Kilgore, *Legal Times*, October 4, 2004.

It is beyond cavil that juveniles as a class are generally less mature, less responsible, and less fully formed than adults, and that these differences bear on juveniles' comparative moral culpability. . . . But even accepting this premise, the Court's proportionality argument fails to support its categorical rule.

Sufficiently Culpable Juveniles

First, the Court adduces no evidence whatsoever in support of its sweeping conclusion that it is only in "rare" cases, if ever, that 17-year-old murderers are sufficiently mature and act with sufficient depravity to warrant the death penalty. The fact that juveniles are generally *less* culpable for their misconduct than adults does not necessarily mean that a 17-year-old murderer cannot be *sufficiently* culpable to merit the death penalty. At most, the Court's argument suggests that the average 17-year-old murderer is not as culpable as the average adult murderer. But an especially depraved juvenile offender may nevertheless be just as culpable as many adult offenders considered bad enough to deserve the death penalty.

Similarly, the fact that the availability of the death penalty may be *less* likely to deter a juvenile from committing a capital crime does not imply that this threat cannot *effectively* deter some 17-year-olds from such an act. Surely there is an age below which no offender, no matter what his crime, can be deemed to have the cognitive or emotional maturity necessary to warrant the death penalty. But at least at the margins between adolescence and adulthood—and especially for 17-year-olds such as respondent—the relevant differences between "adults" and "juveniles" appear to be a matter of degree, rather than of kind. It follows that a legislature may reasonably conclude that at least *some* 17-year-olds can act with sufficient moral culpability, and can be sufficiently deterred by the threat of execution, that capital punishment may be warranted in an appropriate case.

Indeed, this appears to be just such a case. Christopher Simmons' murder of Shirley Crook was premeditated, wanton, and cruel in the extreme. Well before he committed this crime, Simmons declared that he wanted to kill someone. On several occasions, he discussed with two friends (ages 15 and 16) his plan to burglarize a house and to murder the victim by tying the victim up and pushing him from a bridge. Simmons said they could "'get away with it'" because they were minors. . . . In accord with this plan, Simmons and his 15-year-old accomplice broke into Mrs. Crook's home in the middle of the night, forced her from her bed, bound her, and drove her to a state park. There, they walked her to a railroad trestle spanning a river, "hog-tied" her with electrical cable, bound her face completely with duct tape, and pushed her, still alive, from the trestle. She drowned in the water below. One can scarcely imagine the terror that this woman must have suffered throughout the ordeal leading to her death. Whatever can be said about the comparative moral culpability of 17-year-olds as a general matter, Simmons' actions unquestionably reflect "'a consciousness materially more "depraved" than that of' . . . the average murderer." And Simmons' prediction that he could murder with impunity because he had not yet turned 18—though inaccurate—suggests that he *did* take into account the perceived risk of punishment in deciding whether to commit the crime. Based on this evidence, the sentencing jury certainly had reasonable grounds for concluding that, despite Simmons' youth, he "ha[d] sufficient psychological maturity" when he committed this horrific murder, and "at the same time demonstrate[d] sufficient depravity, to merit a sentence of death."

The Maturity of Young Adults

The Court's proportionality argument suffers from a second and closely related defect: It fails to establish that the differences in maturity between 17-year-olds and young "adults" are both universal enough and significant enough to justify a bright-line prophylactic rule against capital punishment of the former. The Court's analysis is premised on differences *in the aggregate* between juveniles and adults, which frequently do not hold true when comparing individuals. Although it may be that many 17-year-old murderers lack sufficient maturity to deserve the death penalty, some juvenile murderers may be quite mature. Chronological age is not an unfailing measure of psychological development, and common experience suggests that many 17-year-olds are more mature than the average young "adult." In short, the class of offenders exempted from capital punishment by today's decision is too broad and too diverse to warrant a categorical prohibition. Indeed, the age-based line drawn by the Court is indefensibly arbitrary—it quite likely will protect a number of offenders who are mature enough to deserve the death penalty and may well leave vulnerable many who are not.

Juveniles Are Different from the Mentally Incapacitated

For purposes of proportionality analysis, 17-year-olds as a class are qualitatively and materially different from the mentally retarded. "Mentally retarded" offenders, as we understood that category in *Atkins*, are *defined* by precisely the characteristics which render death an excessive punishment. A mentally retarded person is, "by definition," one whose cognitive and behavioral capacities have been proven to fall below a certain minimum. Accordingly, for purposes of our decision in *Atkins*, the mentally retarded are not merely *less* blameworthy for their misconduct or *less* likely to be deterred by the death penalty than others. Rather, a mentally retarded offender is one whose demonstrated impairments make it so highly unlikely that he is culpable enough to deserve the death penalty or that he could have been deterred by the threat of death, that execution is not a defensible punishment. There is no such inherent or accurate fit between an offender's chronological age and the personal limitations which the Court believes make capital punishment excessive for 17-year-old murderers. Moreover, it defies common sense to suggest that 17-year-olds as a class are somehow equivalent to mentally retarded persons with regard to culpability or susceptibility to deterrence. Seventeen-year-olds may, on average, be less mature than adults, but that lesser maturity simply cannot be equated with the major, lifelong impairments suffered by the mentally retarded. . . .

The Court argues that sentencing juries cannot accurately evaluate a youthful offender's maturity or give appropriate weight to the mitigating characteristics related to youth. But, again, the Court presents no real evidence—and the record appears to contain none—supporting this claim. Perhaps more importantly, the Court fails to explain why this duty should be so different from, or so much more difficult than, that of assessing and giving proper effect to any other qualitative capital sentencing factor. I would not be so quick to conclude that the constitutional safeguards, the sentencing juries, and the trial judges upon which we place so much reliance in all capital cases are inadequate in this narrow context.

International Opinion

I turn, finally, to the Court's discussion of foreign and international law. Without question, there has been a global trend in recent years towards abolishing capital punishment for under-18 offenders. Very few, if any, countries other than the United States now permit this practice in law or in fact. While acknowledging that the actions and views of other countries do not dictate the outcome of our Eighth Amendment inquiry, the Court asserts that "the overwhelming weight of international opinion against the juvenile death penalty . . . does provide respected and significant confirmation for [its] own conclusions." Because I do not believe that a genuine *national* consensus against the juvenile death penalty has yet developed, and because I do not believe the Court's moral proportionality argument justifies a categorical, age-based constitutional rule, I can assign no such *confirmatory* role to the international consensus described by the Court. In short, the evidence of an international consensus does not alter my determination that the Eighth Amendment does not, at this time, forbid capital punishment of 17-year-old murderers in all cases.

Contemporary Standards of Decency

In determining whether the Eighth Amendment permits capital punishment of a particular offense or class of offenders, we must look to whether such punishment is consistent with contemporary standards of decency. We are obligated to weigh both the objective evidence of societal values and our own judgment as to whether death is an excessive sanction in the context at hand. In the instant case, the objective evidence is inconclusive; standing alone, it does not demonstrate that our society has repudiated capital punishment of 17-year-old offenders in all cases. Rather, the actions of the Nation's legislatures suggest that, although a clear and durable national consensus against this practice may in time emerge, that day has yet to arrive. . . . The Court both pre-empts the democratic debate through which genuine consensus might develop and simultaneously runs a considerable risk of inviting lower court reassessments of our Eighth Amendment precedents.

To be sure, the objective evidence supporting today's decision is similar to (though marginally weaker than) the evidence before the Court in *Atkins*. But *Atkins* could not have been decided as it was based solely on such evidence. Rather, the compelling proportionality argument against capital punishment of the mentally retarded played a decisive role in the Court's Eighth Amendment ruling. Moreover, the constitutional rule adopted in *Atkins* was tailored to this proportionality argument: It exempted from capital punishment a defined group of offenders whose proven impairments rendered it highly unlikely, and perhaps impossible, that they could act with the degree of culpability necessary to deserve death. And *Atkins* left to the States the development of mechanisms to determine which individual offenders fell within this class.

In the instant case, by contrast, the moral proportionality arguments against the juvenile death penalty fail to support the rule the Court adopts today. There is no question that "the chronological age of a minor is itself a relevant mitigating factor of great weight," and that sentencing juries must be given an opportunity carefully to consider a defendant's age and maturity in deciding whether to assess the death penalty. But the mitigating characteristics associated with youth do not justify an absolute age limit. A legislature can reasonably conclude, as many have, that some 17-year-old murderers are mature enough to deserve the death penalty in an appropriate case. And nothing in the record before us suggests that sentencing juries are so unable accurately to assess a 17-year-old defendant's maturity, or so incapable of giving proper weight to youth as a mitigating factor, that the Eighth Amendment requires the bright-line rule imposed today. In the end, the Court's flawed proportionality argument simply cannot bear the weight the Court would place upon it.

The Role of the Legislature

Reasonable minds can differ as to the minimum age at which commission of a serious crime should expose the defendant to the death penalty, if at all. Many jurisdictions have abolished capital punishment altogether, while many others have determined that even the most heinous crime, if committed before the age of 18, should not be punishable by death. Indeed, were my office that of a legislator, rather than a judge, then I, too, would be inclined to support legislation setting a minimum age of 18 in this context. But a significant number of States, including Missouri, have decided to make the death penalty potentially available for 17-year-old capital murderers such as respondent. Without a clearer showing that a genuine national consensus forbids the execution of such offenders, this Court should not substitute its own "inevitably subjective judgment" on how best to resolve this difficult moral question for the judgments of the Nation's democratically elected legislatures.

*"Advances in DNA technology hold
enormous potential to enhance our quality
of justice even more dramatically."*

DNA Evidence Will Make the Death Penalty More Fair

Paul A. Logli

In the following viewpoint, originally given as testimony to
the U.S. Senate Judiciary Committee, Paul A. Logli claims
that DNA evidence will make the justice system more fair.
He maintains that with DNA evidence, prosecutors can often establish the guilt of defendants conclusively. Logli argues that DNA testing should be used primarily before trials to ensure justice; postconviction DNA testing should be
used only in cases where the defendant was sent to prison or
death row before DNA testing was available. Logli is a state's
attorney from Winnebago County, Illinois.

As you read, consider the following questions:
1. Describe Logli's jurisdiction.
2. What does Logli ask the legislature to do and why?
3. In Logli's opinion what are three popular misconceptions
   concerning DNA testing?

Paul A. Logli, testimony before the U.S. Senate Committee on the Judiciary,
Washington, DC, June 18, 2002.

My name is Paul Logli and I am the elected state's attorney in Winnebago County, Illinois. I want to thank you, on behalf of the National District Attorneys Association, for the opportunity to present our position on DNA testing in post-conviction settings and share some thoughts on the issue of counsel competency. The views that I express today represent the views of that Association and the beliefs of thousands of local prosecutors across this country.

To place my remarks in context—let me briefly tell you about my jurisdiction. Winnebago County is located about 70 miles west of Chicago. It has a population of nearly 280,000 people living in a diverse community. The county seat is Rockford—the second largest city in the state. I have been a prosecutor for 18 years and am honored to have served in my current position for 16 years, having been elected to office 4 times. I previously served as a judge of the local circuit court for nearly 6 years. I currently supervise a staff that includes 38 assistant state's attorneys. Annually, my office handles about 4000 felony cases.

I want to emphasize to the Committee that as a prosecutor I represent the only trial attorneys in the United States whose primary ethical obligation is to seek the truth wherever it takes us. I, as well as all local prosecutors, support the use of DNA technology in catching criminals, convicting the guilty and identifying the truly innocent. . . .

DNA Testing in the Criminal Justice System

Our Association has consistently embraced DNA technology as a scientific breakthrough in the search for truth. Since the mid-1980s, when DNA evidence was first introduced we have fought for its admission in criminal trials and we have been instrumental in providing training to prosecutors on using DNA evidence in investigations and in the courtroom. With the use of DNA evidence, prosecutors are often able to conclusively establish the guilt of a defendant in cases where identity is at issue. Prosecutors and law enforcement agencies also utilize DNA technologies to eliminate suspects and exonerate the innocent. It is our view that this powerful weapon against the criminal offender is best used when such resources are made fully available in the earliest stages of an investigation and before a conviction.

Forensic DNA typing has had a broad, positive impact on the criminal justice system. In recent years, convictions have been obtained that previously would have been impossible. Countless suspects have been eliminated prior to the filing of charges. Old, unsolved criminal cases, as well as new cases, have been solved. In a very few cases, mistakenly accused defendants have been freed both before trial and after incarceration. Increasingly, the unidentified remains of crime victims are being identified.

Advances in DNA technology hold enormous potential to enhance our quality of justice even more dramatically. However, significant increases in resources are needed to enlarge forensic laboratory capacity and expand DNA databases. No other investment in our criminal justice system will do more to protect the innocent, convict the guilty and reduce human suffering.

In keeping with these beliefs, the National District Attorneys Association has supported funding for forensic laboratories to eliminate backlogs in the testing of biological samples from convicted offenders and crime scenes. Funding by the federal government is a critical component in realizing the full potential of DNA testing. Federal funding should not be contingent upon a state's adoption of any specific federally mandated and unfunded legislation such as post conviction relief standards. . . .

We will continue to support legislative efforts to provide funding support for state forensic laboratories, an example of which is our association's support of Senator [Joseph] Biden's efforts to eliminate the unconscionable backlog of untested rape kits in police department evidence rooms across this country.

Support for DNA Testing

The National District Attorneys Association has always supported the use of DNA testing where such testing will prove the actual innocence of a previously convicted individual and not serve as a diversionary attack on the conviction.

First, we need to clear up several popular misconceptions. The vast majority of criminal cases do not involve DNA evidence. Just as fingerprint evidence, although available for decades, is seldom a conclusive factor in a prosecution, DNA evidence will likewise, even though it is increasingly available and more determinative, will not be a factor in a large majority of cases.

Secondly, the absence of a biological sample, in and of itself, is not necessarily dispositive of innocence. There can be many reasons why an identifiable biological sample was not available at a crime scene, yet an individual can still be guilty of the commission of a crime. In many cases DNA testing results that exclude an individual as the donor of biological evidence do not exonerate a suspect as innocent. In a sexual assault involving multiple perpetrators, for example, a defendant may have participated in the rape without depositing identified DNA evidence. In such cases, the absence of a sample or a comparative exclusion is not synonymous with exoneration. Moreover, as powerful as DNA evidence is, it tells us nothing about issues such as consent, self-defense or the criminal intent of the perpetrator.

Lastly, the issue of post-conviction DNA testing, such as contemplated by the Innocence Protection Act, involves only cases prosecuted before adequate DNA technology existed. In the future, the need for post-conviction DNA testing should cease because of the availability of pretrial testing with advanced technology. Thus, while the debate is important, we are examining a finite number of cases whose numbers are dwindling.

Limiting Post-Conviction DNA Testing

We believe that post-conviction DNA testing, in most cases, should be afforded only where such testing was not previously available to the defendant. Post-conviction testing should be employed only in those cases where a result favorable to the defendant establishes proof of the defendant's actual innocence, exonerating the defendant as the perpetrator or accomplice to the crime.

In limited circumstances post-conviction DNA testing may be appropriate where testing previously has been performed. Although DNA testing in criminal cases became available in the mid-1980s, the forms of testing typically used today were not widely available until the mid-1990s. These present-day methodologies allow the testing of much smaller samples in a shorter time and are reliable on degraded samples.

Ensuring Justice and Fairness for All Americans

An important part of the American character is our system of justice, and we have a solemn obligation to make sure that cases involving the death penalty have been handled in full accordance with all the guarantees of our Constitution. The foundations of America's democracy depend on the assurance of fairness in our legal system.

The President is committed to ensuring justice and fairness in America's legal system by providing full funding for the use of DNA evidence to solve crime and prevent wrongful convictions. . . .

American unity is strengthened by our confident belief in a fair and accurate legal system.

DNA technology can be vital in ensuring accuracy and fairness in the criminal justice system. DNA can be used to identify criminals with incredible accuracy when biological evidence exists, and DNA can be used to clear suspects and exonerate persons mistakenly accused or convicted of crimes.

"Ensuring Justice and Fairness for All Americans," Fact Sheet, The White House, February 2, 2005.

Because of these considerations the National District Attorneys Association has consistently supported state legislation that removes barriers to post-conviction DNA testing in appropriate cases and with appropriate safeguards.

We recognize that in some states, legislative enactment of new legal remedies may be required to provide post-conviction DNA testing. Many states have enacted such legislation, and others are considering such measures. The NDAA supports enabling legislation that addresses concerns of prosecutors and victims, such as avoiding frivolous litigation and preserving necessary finality in the criminal justice system. These statutes should provide for the inclusion in the national CODIS [Combined DNA Index System] database of DNA profiles obtained as a result of post-conviction

DNA testing. This provision will help to solve crimes and deter abuses of the post-conviction relief mechanism. . . .

Time Limits on DNA Testing

The resources for DNA testing are finite. Conducting frivolous or non-conclusive tests could mean that another test freeing an innocent person or apprehending a guilty person would not be done in a timely manner or at all.

The National District Attorneys Association believes that post-conviction relief remedies must protect against potential abuse and that such remedies must respect the importance of finality in the criminal justice system. Thus, such remedies should be subject to limits on the period in which relief may be sought.

Current prohibitions limiting post-conviction relief are grounded in legitimate policy, enhancing the search for the truth and minimizing potential abuse. The defense, for example, should be expected to exercise due diligence in developing and presenting all legally appropriate exonerating or mitigating evidence to the trial jury. Potentially exonerating evidence should be actively pursued. A trial jury's verdict should be accorded great weight and normally should be overturned only where harmful legal error has occurred or an innocent person convicted. The peace of mind of a crime victim or crime victim's family should not be frivolously disturbed by a lack of finality arising from post-conviction relief remedies. For these reasons, any initiatives to identify and exonerate the innocent should also protect against abuses.

Time limits on the period in which post-conviction relief may be sought provide one of the most important means to ensure finality in the criminal justice system. Post-conviction relief remedies are needed only for a relatively small group of cases prosecuted before present-day DNA technology existed. Reasonable time limits on the consideration of these cases should not interfere with due process for convicted individuals who may seek relief.

Law enforcement should be permitted to destroy biological samples from closed cases, provided that convicted individuals are given adequate notice and opportunity to request testing. Otherwise, police agencies and the courts would be required to retain virtually all evidence for all time.

NDAA also support the decisions of individual prosecution offices to initiate post-conviction DNA testing programs. Such programs can serve to strengthen public confidence in the criminal justice system.

In summary, any post-conviction DNA testing program should focus only on those cases where identity is an issue and where testing would, assuming exculpatory results, establish the actual innocence of an individual. Such programs should recognize the need for finality in criminal justice proceedings by establishing a limited time period in which cases will be considered and then reviewing those cases in an expedited manner.

"Evidence presented under the veil of scientific certainty becomes the very source of misinformation leading to mistake."

DNA Evidence Does Not Make the Death Penalty More Fair

Richard Dieter

In the following viewpoint Richard Dieter refutes the notion that DNA evidence will make the death penalty more fair. Dieter asserts that DNA evidence is frequently mishandled by some labs due to unqualified personnel, understaffed facilities, and improper techniques. As a result, the reliability of DNA evidence varies widely from lab to lab, disadvantaging people who live in some jurisdictions. Finally, because juries place so much weight on forensic testimony, DNA evidence, no matter how badly handled, unfairly influences jury decisions. Dieter has been the executive director of the Death Penalty Information Center since 1992.

As you read, consider the following questions:
1. What forms of evidence are most commonly used to exonerate prisoners, according to Dieter?
2. Why did the mayor of Houston call for a moratorium on all executions, according to the author?
3. What are some of the specific problems Dieter cites with DNA lab personnel in Houston?

Richard Dieter, "Innocence and the Crisis in the American Death Penalty," www.deathpenaltyinfo.org, September 2004. Copyright © 2004 by the Death Penalty Information Center. Reproduced by permission.

The era of DNA testing has not ushered in a fool-proof criminal justice system. It is not true that the problems of wrongful convictions are in the past and will not happen anymore because technology can now precisely determine guilt. Nor is it true that the death penalty can proceed unchecked under the assumption that all the inmates on death row have had ample opportunity for DNA testing.

To begin with, exonerations from death row have not declined in recent years. In fact, the number of people that were freed in 2003 was more than in any year since death sentencing resumed in 1973. Twelve people were cleared of their original offense in 2003. Moreover, the average number of exonerations has steadily increased in each quarter of the total years covered in this report: 1973–2004.

The Importance of Other Evidence

Only 14 of these exonerations have been due to DNA testing. It is true that more states now allow this kind of new evidence to be tested and admitted on appeal, despite time limitations on appeals. However, the DNA exonerations represent only 12% of the total list of 116 cases. In 88% of the cases, attorneys and courts had to rely on other forms of evidence, such as a confession by the actual killer, witnesses who now admit that they were pressured into lying at trial, or the refinement of other kinds of forensic testing such as fingerprint or bite mark analysis.

There is no reason to believe that all of the innocent people among the 3,500 people on death row have been discovered. Some states like Alabama do not supply attorneys for the complete appeals process. In other states, the attorneys do not have the resources for adequate re-investigation. In California, death row inmates wait four years to be assigned an attorney to begin the appeals process, and often several more years until counsel to pursue habeas corpus proceedings is appointed. In that intervening time, witnesses move, evidence is lost, and memories fade.

Many states have not passed legislation guaranteeing the right to DNA testing. Even where this right is protected by statute, such as in Texas, there are stringent limits on its use and inmates have been refused testing where the results might have affected the death sentence, even if not the determination of their guilt.

The Reliability of DNA Evidence

But what of the new cases coming into the system? Shouldn't DNA testing ensure that only the guilty are being convicted and sentenced to death? This is not the case because most murders do not involve the exchange of bodily materials containing DNA evidence. A single shooting where no blood of the victim appears on the perpetrator and the defendant drives away in his own car is not likely to be a DNA case. And yet, the same kind of errors that have arisen in DNA cases—faulty eyewitnesses, unreliable jailhouse snitch testimony, coerced confessions, withheld evidence of other suspects—can just as easily arise in non-DNA cases. Wrongful convictions will continue to occur as long as our criminal justice system utilizes human actors. Exonerations due to DNA testing only serve to underscore the risk of mistake in every case.

When newly tested DNA evidence is presented after an inmate has been convicted and sentenced to death, it is usually checked and rechecked before that inmate is ever set free. However, it appears that the same reliability cannot be attributed to the *pre-trial* DNA testing that can often result in a conviction and a death sentence. Recent scandals from crime labs in many parts of the country have exposed the risk of wrongful convictions that shoddy forensic work can bring.

The performance of pre-trial DNA testing is not always a reliable source of forensic information. If evidence is contaminated at the scene of the crime, if the police are not skilled in the collection of such evidence, if the police lab that performs the testing is unqualified to render reliable results, or if the state's expert is incompetent or dishonest, then evidence presented under the veil of scientific certainty becomes the very source of misinformation leading to mistake.

The Example of Harris County, Texas

Recent developments in Harris County (Houston), Texas are perhaps the most shocking example of such dereliction. More executions occur in cases from Harris County than from most other *states* in the country. The DNA testing in

Human Error

DNA evidence is . . . subject to human error. Confidence in many testing labs has been shaken by confirmed cases of botched, falsified, and otherwise erroneous procedures, most infamously at the Houston Police Department crime laboratory, where a 17-year-old boy was convicted for rape based on improperly processed DNA samples.

Brian Handwerk, *National Geographic News*, April 8, 2005.

the crime lab there has proven so unreliable that all of its results are being stricken from the national database of DNA profiles. The roof at the lab has been leaking for years, contaminating critical evidence. The mayor of Houston has called for a moratorium on all executions in cases from that city, and he has decided not to seek re-election in the wake of the scandal. Two grand juries have been convened to look into the scandal. And it appears that other forms of forensic evidence, such as ballistics tests, have likewise been mishandled by the lab.

Unqualified Personnel

An investigation by the *Houston Chronicle* into personnel assigned to the lab revealed:

- The founder and former head of the DNA lab, James Bolding, did not meet the standards for the job. Among other things, he originally failed both algebra and geometry in college, and he never took statistics. Bolding held a bachelor's and a master's degree from Texas Southern University, but was academically dismissed from the University of Texas Ph.D. program. Bolding resigned from the lab after Houston's police chief recommended he be fired.
- Jobs were often given to graduates without the required degrees, such as those who had majored in chemistry or zoology. Among those hired to do DNA tests or prepare samples for testing were two workers from the city zoo. One had most recently been cleaning elephant cages. The other had done DNA research, but only on insects.
- The lab hired Joseph Chu despite a former employer's comment that he "has difficulty in speaking English" (a

serious handicap when testifying in court). In his application, he wrote, "I have skilled several equipments" and "I have experience in testing animal and sacrificing them." His supervisors rated him poorly in communication. Chu was suspended for 14 days after several errors were found in four cases, including a capital murder case. He also misrepresented his degree in a court document.

The Reliance on DNA Evidence Is Misplaced

The importance of these events is greatly heightened when their role in the death penalty arena is considered. Texas leads the country by far in executions. About 35% of the executions in the modern era have occurred in Texas, three times as many as the next leading state. And Harris County is the leading jurisdiction in Texas in executions. Juries there, as elsewhere, put enormous weight on the sworn testimony of forensic experts who confidently link evidence to a particular defendant on trial. But reliance on that evidence is sadly misplaced.

Hundreds of cases are being reviewed including that of Josiah Sutton, who was convicted of rape but has now been freed and pardoned by the governor. The problems with DNA labs are not confined to Houston. Concerns have also been raised about Texas labs in Fort Worth. In Oklahoma, which is currently close to Texas for the most executions, the chief police chemist, Joyce Gilchrist, was fired from her position after an FBI investigation of her lab. Again, hundreds of cases are being reviewed, including many where the defendants are awaiting execution. And around the country, there are reports of improper testing techniques and erroneous testimony at labs in Arizona, Florida, and other states. The FBI's lab has also come under withering criticism and has been completely restructured.

Demanding qualified personnel, establishing standards for forensic labs, creating an oversight mechanism to ensure quality, all will take time to implement. But in the meantime, people who were put on death row as a result of testimony by unqualified witnesses are often at the mercy of review by the same authorities that allowed such a scandal to develop in the first place. A fair review of these cases in court is not necessarily guaranteed, as the debacle in Texas shows. Houston's District Attorney, Chuck Rosenthal, refused to recuse himself from the investigation of the city's lab, despite numerous calls from editorials, the mayor, and former prosecutors. The grand juries investigating the scandal had to insist that they would operate on their own, without the usual input from the prosecutor's office.

"An attorney who is mediocre, overworked, careless, or without funds . . . can let someone . . . slip into the execution chamber."

Attorney Incompetence Makes the Death Penalty Unfair

Friends Committee on Legislation Education Fund

The members of the Friends Committee on Legislation Education Fund (FCLEF) contend in the following viewpoint that despite California's high standards governing public defenders, many defendants receive inferior legal representation, often leading to an unfair conviction and sentence. The FCLEF argues that anyone being investigated for murder needs superior legal counsel immediately because his or her life is at stake. Too often, however, public defenders and court-appointed attorneys have neither the skill nor experience to adequately represent their clients. Thus, people without money who must have court-appointed attorneys are in greater jeopardy of wrongful conviction than are wealthier defendants, the FCLEF asserts. The FCLEF is a nonprofit action group working on social justice issues.

As you read, consider the following questions:
1. What are the differences between a superior lawyer and a mediocre lawyer, according to the FCLEF?
2. What are some of the factors that erode the credibility of the criminal justice system, according to the FCLEF?
3. What are some of the problems the FCLEF cites with attorneys who represent defendants in death penalty cases?

Friends Committee on Legislation Education Fund, "The Death Penalty and Attorneys," www.fclca.org, July 4, 2001. Copyright © 2001 by the Friends Committee on Legislation and Education. Reproduced by permission.

California still does not assure all murder defendants adequate representation, and there is reason to doubt that we will ever do so. Capital cases place such high demands on lawyers and judges, and the number of death eligible cases is so large that the existence of the death penalty will always pose a risk that a defendant will be poorly represented. Many of the mistakes lawyers make cannot be corrected by the appellate courts.

Compared with many states, California has high standards for public defenders. But regardless of their skill and dedication, these lawyers have limited resources, and they cannot represent all defendants in death cases. In 1998, public defense personnel accounted for 2% of criminal justice personnel while prosecution personnel accounted for 8.6%. More strikingly, from 1993 to 1998, prosecution personnel increased 53.8%, while defense personnel increased only 11.6%.

California law says that a person facing a possible death sentence may have two attorneys at state expense, but it does not guarantee the accused an excellent lawyer. Also, a lawyer might not be appointed until the police investigation is nearly complete, and charges have been brought against a suspect, placing the accused person at a serious disadvantage.

Superior vs. Mediocre Lawyers

An excellent lawyer may prevent a client from receiving the death penalty, even when charged with a heinous offense. A superior lawyer will be able to continually remind the police, the prosecutor, and the media, that the accused is a human being and entitled to respect, no matter how serious the offense may appear to be. But an attorney who is mediocre, overworked, careless, or without funds to retain the best expert witnesses or investigators can let someone charged with a much less egregious killing slip into the execution chamber.

Anyone under investigation for homicide needs expert legal advice right away. For example, evidence that could distinguish a case of manslaughter or second degree murder from first degree murder needs to be preserved. Facts that could show self-defense or the mental state of the individuals involved must not be lost. If the accused is in custody, he or she needs protection from cell-mates who might assert the suspect confessed to the crime.

Flaws in California's System

The flaws in California's system of justice were underlined twice last year [2000] by the release of prisoners mistakenly convicted of murder. In February, Dwayne McKinney, who had spent 20 years behind bars after a wrongful conviction for murdering a Burger King manager, was finally cleared by new evidence. The Orange County district attorney had sought the death penalty. His life was spared because the jury decided instead on life without possibility of parole. In May, David Quindt, who had been wrongly convicted of a home invasion murder, was freed after Sacramento prosecutors obtained confessions implicating three other suspects in the crime.

The Necessity of Post-Conviction Review

Post-conviction review is crucial: It is the method of ensuring that capital trials are fair and that death sentences are appropriate. It is a proceeding intended to prevent wrongful executions, to find any new evidence proving innocence and to root out cases of prosecutorial misconduct, shoddy police work, mistaken eye-witnesses, false confessions and sleeping trial lawyers. But when inadequate lawyers and unaccountable courts sacrifice meaningful post-conviction review for speed and finality, death sentences are unreliable because mistakes are not caught and corrected.

Texas Defender Service, "Lethal Indifference," 2002. www.texasdefender.org.

Cases like McKinney and Quindt undermine the myth that defendants in California are adequately protected by dedicated public defenders or by counsel appointed by judges who understand the importance of avoiding errors at the trial. Several factors erode the credibility of the criminal justice system:

- Some people in communities of color don't trust public defenders and regard them as a part of the criminal justice bureaucracy that oppresses them.
- Often, the family of the accused scrapes together all the money they can to hire private counsel, but they can't afford a good investigation, or the defense that is most likely to produce a fair result.

- Public defenders and contract lawyers who defend accused murderers must often operate on a shoestring budget. There is a shortage of defense investigators to locate evidence while the case is hot, and a shortage of experienced lawyers to defend capital cases, yet staffing for district attorneys tends to increase much more quickly than public defender staffing.
- As recent revelations of official corruption in the Los Angeles Police Department and elsewhere demonstrate, perjured police testimony needs to be reckoned with in California's criminal courts. It is very time consuming for defense counsel to cope with such issues effectively; few are equal to the task.
- Under California law, once a verdict is handed down, the defense loses its ability to discover new evidence that might uncover a mistake. Therefore, many instances of ineffective assistance may go undiscovered.

Problems with Attorneys

Cost: Legal advice is essential for any suspect, from the very start of a homicide investigation, yet few people can afford to hire a lawyer who is experienced in such cases. The result is that during the initial, and sometimes critical stages of the case, poor suspects get no legal advice on whether they should submit to interviews, tests and lineups and on the kinds of evidence that should be brought to the attention of the district attorney. They usually hope for the best, wait to see whether the police investigation results in a charge against them, and then have a lawyer appointed for them at public expense. Unless the public defender steps into the investigation, perishable evidence can be lost, individuals may be wrongly charged, and it can be hard to prevent false or misleading evidence from affecting the case.

Competence: Sometimes a suspect who is not wealthy will hire a private attorney, either due to mistrust of court-appointed lawyers, or on the recommendation of a friend. The result can be disastrous. The lawyer may have underestimated the risks in the case, and over-estimate his or her own ability. The client may have scraped together a $20,000 retainer, promising more if necessary, and the lawyer may expect the case to settle early in the process. By the time it becomes clear that the district attorney is asking for the death penalty, important evidence may have been lost. Serious injustice can result.

Dedication: The public defenders' offices cannot handle all homicide cases, and so private lawyers are often appointed on a per diem basis. Because they are not specifically trained or supervised in handling homicide cases, the quality and dedication of these lawyers can vary greatly. A few private lawyers take murder cases to put bread on the table for their families; some may think their client deserves the death penalty, and some neglect to request enough investigation time to prepare a spirited defense.

Funding: Budgets for public defender services are always tight, and there are never enough investigators to meet the needs of all defendants. Often, assigned attorneys must justify proposed investigative work to a judge. In these circumstances, it is easy for lawyers and investigators to pre-judge the guilt or innocence of a client, and to focus resources accordingly. Clients who cannot convince their own advocates of their innocence may lose out.

Examples of Botched Cases

In California, Shasta County prosecutors dropped their death penalty case against Thomas Brewster in mid-trial when the defense presented DNA evidence which excluded the defendant. Brewster was on trial for a 1985 murder and sexual assault. A piece of clothing from one of the victims had never been tested for DNA, despite having been sent to the State's lab on two occasions. The prosecution dropped all charges because they became convinced that Brewster was innocent. He had been in jail for 2 years awaiting trial.

Lee Perry Farmer was acquitted at a re-trial in California of capital murder. He had spent 9 years on death row. He was, however, convicted of burglary and being an accessory to murder. He was credited with time already served and will be released. A federal court had overturned his first conviction because of incompetent counsel. Another man confessed to the murder.

"The past few decades have seen the establishment of public defender systems that in many cases rival some of the best lawyers retained privately."

Attorney Competence Does Not Make the Death Penalty Unfair

Joshua K. Marquis

In the following viewpoint excerpted from testimony before the U.S. House Subcommittee on Crime and Terrorism, Joshua K. Marquis argues that the charge of ill-prepared and underfunded indigent defense attorneys is an urban legend spread by death penalty abolitionists. He maintains that defense attorneys are both competent and receive adequate funding to mount effective defenses. According to Marquis, improvements in the judicial system have led to a decrease in death penalty sentences and an increase in fairness. Joshua K. Marquis is a district attorney in Clatsop County, Oregon.

As you read, consider the following questions:

1. According to Marquis, why do those who oppose the death penalty call themselves abolitionists?
2. What did the *Chicago Tribune* have to say about the Cook County Public Defender's Office, according to Marquis?
3. In Marquis' opinion, what has been the response of death penalty abolitionists to public support for the death penalty?

Joshua K. Marquis, testimony before the U.S. House Subcommittee on Crime and Terrorism, Committee on the Judiciary, Washington, DC, June 30, 2005.

For decades in America questions about the death penalty centered on philosophical and sometimes religious debate over the morality of the state-sanctioned execution of another human being. Public opinion ebbed and flowed with support for the death penalty declining as civil rights abuses became a national concern in the 1960s and increasing along with a rapid rise in violent crime in the 1980s.

Changing the Focus

Those who oppose capital punishment call themselves "abolitionists," clearly relishing the comparison to those who fought slavery in the 19th century. In the mid 1990s these abolitionists . . . succeeded in changing the focus of the debate over the death penalty from the morality of executions to questions about the "fundamental fairness" or, in their minds, unfairness of the institution. The abolitionists were frustrated by polling that showed that virtually all groups of Americans supported capital punishment in some form in some cases. . . .

[O]pponents of capital punishment undertook a sweeping make-over of their campaign. In addition to painting America as a rogue state, a wolf among the peaceful lambs of the European Union who had forsaken the death penalty, the latter-day abolitionists sought to convince America that as carried out the death penalty was inherently racist, that the unfortunates on death row received wretched and often incompetent defense counsel, and, most appalling, that a remarkable number of those sentenced to death were in fact innocent.

Abolitionist Charges

[Abolitionists] pointed to the fact that while African-Americans make up only slightly more than 10 percent of the American population, they constitute more than 40 percent of those on death row. They described cases in which the lawyers appointed to represent someone facing execution were in some cases nothing more than golfing pals with the judge making the appointment, that some of these lawyers had no previous experience with murder cases, and that in at least one case the lawyer appears to have slept through portions of the trial.

Abolitionists painted a picture of massive prosecution, funded by the endless resources of the government pitted against threadbare public defenders either barely out of law school or, if experienced, pulled from the rubbish heap of the legal profession. . . .

Incompetent Defense: An Urban Legend

The . . . threadbare but plucky public defender fighting against all odds against a team of sleek, heavily-funded prosecutors with limitless resources [is an urban legend]. The reality in the 21st century is startlingly different. There is no doubt that before the landmark 1963 decision in *Gideon vs. Wainwright*, appointed counsel was often inadequate. But the past few decades have seen the establishment of public defender systems that in many cases rival some of the best lawyers retained privately. The *Chicago Tribune*, while slamming the abilities of a number of individual defense counsel in capital cases in the 1980s in Cook County, grudgingly admitted that the Cook County Public Defender's Office provided excellent representation for its indigent clients.

Many giant silk-stocking law firms in large cities across America not only provide pro-bono counsel in capital cases, they also offer partnerships to lawyers whose sole job is to promote indigent capital defense. In one recent case in Alabama, a Portland, Oregon law firm spent hundreds of thousands of dollars of lawyer time on a post-conviction appeal for a death row inmate. In Oregon, where I have both prosecuted and defended capital cases, it is common for attorneys to be paid hundreds of thousands of dollars by the state for their representation of indigent capital clients. And the funding is not limited to legal assistance. Expert witnesses for the defense often total tens of thousands of dollars each, resources far beyond the reach of individual district attorneys who prosecute the same cases.

As the elected prosecutor of what is considered a midsized county in Oregon, I have a set budget that rarely gives me more than $15,000 a year to cover the total expenses of expert witnesses for ALL the hundreds of cases my office prosecutes each year. Yet in one recent murder trial one witness in the mitigation phase admitted he had already billed the state indigent defense program for over $30,000. In a related case the investigators for the defense were paid over $100,000. . . .

Super Due Process

The justice system is far from perfect and has made many mistakes, mostly in *favor* of the accused. Hundreds if not thousands have died or lost their livelihoods through embezzlement or rape because the American justice system failed to incarcerate people who were guilty by any definition.

Since the death penalty was re-authorized in 1976 by the Supreme Court, there have been upwards of 500,000 murders. About 7,000 murderers were sentenced to death and about 3,700 remain on death row today. Seven hundred and fifty have been executed. Appellate courts at the state and federal levels have imposed what one justice called "super due process" for convicted capital murderers, overturning almost two-thirds of all death sentences, a rate far exceeding that in other cases. Virtually none have been overturned because of "actual innocence."

Some claim that a civilized society must be prepared to allow ten guilty men to walk free in order to spare one innocent. But the well-organized and even better-funded abolitionists cannot point to a single case of a demonstrably innocent person executed in the modern era of American capital punishment.

Victims of the Freed

Instead, let's tally the *additional* victims of the freed:

Nine, killed by Kenneth McDuff, who had been sentenced to die for child murder in Texas and then was freed on parole after the death penalty laws at the time were overturned.

One, by Robert Massie of California, also sentenced to die and also paroled. Massie rewarded the man who gave him a job on parole by murdering him less than a year after getting out of prison.

One, by Richard Marquette, in Oregon, sentenced to "life" (which until 1994 meant about eight years in Oregon) for abducting and then dismembering women. He did so well in a woman-free environment (prison) that he was released—only to abduct, kill and dismember women again.

Two, by Carl Cletus Bowles, in Idaho, guilty of kidnapping nine people and the murder of a police officer. Bowles escaped during a conjugal visit with a girlfriend, only to abduct and murder an elderly couple.

High-Quality Representation

Defendants charged with capital offenses in California receive high-quality representation. . . . Often, capital defendants retain leading experts in the scientific community to testify in their cases. Whenever a sentence of death is imposed, California law provides an automatic appeal to the state Supreme Court. At this stage, additional skilled and experienced attorneys are appointed to represent the defendant. If the state appeal is unsuccessful, another set of attorneys is appointed to take the case to federal court.

Michael D. Bradbury, *Los Angeles Times*, September 24, 2000.

The victims of these men didn't have "close calls" with death. They are dead. Murdered. Without saying goodbye to their loved ones. Without appeal to the state or the media or Hollywood or anyone's heartstrings.

Abolitionist Strategy

Discouraged over polls that have consistently shown public support for capital punishment between 65 and 85 percent over the last quarter century, proponents of the death penalty have decided to tap into an understandable horror that people who are truly innocent of the murder of which they stand convicted are on death row. They are turning into doe-eyed innocents the few murderers who have slipped through one of the countless cracks in the law afforded to capital defendants. They want us to believe that any one of us could be snatched at any time from our daily freedoms and sentenced to die because of a false and coerced confession, police corruption, faulty eyewitness identification, botched forensics, prosecutorial misconduct, and shoddy and ill-paid defense counsel.

There are a handful of people who have spent time, in some cases many years, on death row, for crimes they genuinely did not commit. The number bandied about by the abolitionists just passed the 100 mark. But a closer examination using a more realistic definition of innocence—that is, had no involvement in the death, wasn't there, didn't do it—drops the number to 30 or even 25. At a seminar in February of 2004 held by the Federal Bar Council of New York, US District Court Judge Jed Rakoff, who made history in 2001 by ruling the death penalty unconstitutional, acknowledged that his research showed the number to be closer to 30. The larger question is whether the problem of wrongful convictions in capital cases is an episodic or epidemic problem.

For those who believe that no rate of error is acceptable, the death penalty can never be "reformed" sufficiently, despite the claims that they are seeking only to insure a fairer system. Yet these same advocates urge the substitution of life without parole, claiming (as is sometimes true) that many inmates consider a life sentence to be worse than execution. Peel back the layers of this reckoning and you'll find these advocates claiming that it is just as horrible to threaten to take away the remaining days of a murderer's life, and therefore we must abolish all long prison sentences as well as the death penalty.

Improvements in the System

The number of death sentences is, in fact, decreasing. Criminal sentences for crimes other than murder have become tougher, terms of imprisonment more certain, and perhaps more significantly, the rate of murder is down overall. Prosecutors and juries are properly and appropriately becoming even more discriminating about determining who should die for their crimes. It is a journey not taken lightly.

Likewise, casting the accused as true innocents caught up by a corrupt and uncaring system only discredits a movement that has legitimate moral arguments. Nothing excuses making the victims nameless and faceless, making martyrs out of murderers, and turning killers into victims.

Periodical Bibliography

The following articles have been selected to supplement the diverse views presented in this chapter.

America	"Innocence and the Death Penalty," February 7, 2005.
American Bar Association	"*Gideon*'s Broken Promise: America's Continuing Quest for Equal Justice," Report on the American Bar Association's Hearings on the Right to Counsel in Criminal Proceedings, December 2004. www.indigentdefense.org.
Bruce C. Bower	"Teen Brains on Trial," *Science News*, May 8, 2004.
James Dao	"Lab Errors in '82 Killing Force Review of Virginia DNA Cases," *New York Times*, May 7, 2005.
Michael Hall	"Death Isn't Fair," *Texas Monthly*, December 2002.
Mary Klein	"DNA Science Mandates a Death Penalty Moratorium," *Palo Alto Weekly*, June 26, 2002. www.paloaltoonline.com.
Andre M. Lee	"Rationale for an Execution Moratorium," *Corrections Today*, October 2003.
M. Marshall	"JLARC Study Finds No Racial Bias in Virginia Death Penalty Sentencing," University of Virginia Law Home Page, 2002. www.law.virginia.
David Mote	"Defending the Defense Against Post-Moratorium Fallout," *Back Bench*, February 2000.
Susan L. Pollet	"The Juvenile Death Penalty," *New York Law Journal*, October 13, 2004.
Bill Pryor	"Alabama Executes Only the Guilty," Alabama Attorney General Home Page, July 2000. www.ago.state.al.us.
Lois Romano	"When DNA Meets Death Row, It's the System That's Tested," *Washington Post*, December 12, 2003.
Jeffrey Rosen	"Juvenile Logic," *New Republic*, March 21, 2005.
Sally Satel and Christina Sommers	"Brain-Based Leniency Would Give Teen Killers a Pass," *USA Today*, April 22, 2005.
Seth Stern	"Can You Build a Foolproof Death Penalty?" *Christian Science Monitor*, November 5, 2003.
Joseph D. Tidings	"Too Young to Die? Yes," *Legal Times*, October 4, 2004.

CHAPTER 4

Should the Death Penalty Be Reformed?

Chapter Preface

In the first years of the twenty-first century, thirteen men sitting on death row in Illinois, awaiting what they thought was their inevitable execution, were exonerated, largely through the use of DNA evidence, a technology not available when most of them were originally tried. In 2000, when the thirteenth man was released from prison, Illinois governor George Ryan decided to stop all executions in his state, stating, "Until I can be sure that no innocent man or woman is facing lethal injection, no one will meet that fate." His goal in establishing the moratorium was to create a commission that would examine the death penalty and make recommendations for its reform. When Ryan left office in 2003, he commuted death sentences for all 156 prisoners on death row in Illinois.

In April 2002 the Illinois Commission on Capital Punishment issued a long list of reforms, including new procedures for handling eyewitness testimony, a mandatory Illinois Supreme Court review of all death sentences, and the videotaping of the interrogation of homicide suspects. Some of the commission's recommendations have been passed into law; however, present-day governor Rod Blagojevich has maintained the moratorium.

Other states have followed Illinois in reconsidering the death penalty. The state of Maryland, for example, instituted a moratorium on the death penalty in 2002 but lifted the ban in early 2003. The state of New York abandoned the death penalty in April 2005 after conducting state assembly hearings in January of that year. In April 2005 Massachusetts governor Mitt Romney called for both reinstatement and reform of his state's death penalty laws. He introduced a bill to the state legislature that he said would be "the gold standard" for the death penalty. At the core of his reform is the use of DNA evidence to make sure that guilt is established accurately. Massachusetts lawmakers have not yet acted on Romney's proposed legislation.

State efforts to reform or abolish the death penalty would seem to suggest a public steeply divided over the issue. However, according to a May 2005 Gallup poll, there is strong support for the continuation of the death penalty: Seventy-four percent of those surveyed support the death penalty while only 23 percent are not in favor. Further, the 2005 poll shows that more people believe the death penalty is applied fairly than they did in a 2003 poll. At the same time, the number of executions carried out nationally continues to fall.

For some people, issues of error and innocence are the most essential components of the death penalty debate. For others, it is a matter of economics. The writers of the viewpoints in the following chapter consider various ways the death penalty could be reformed.

"*Our position . . . is that there is no place for capital punishment. . . . We believe that justice for all is better served by a sentence of life imprisonment.*"

The Death Penalty Should Be Abolished

Women's Bar Association of the State of New York

The Women's Bar Association of the State of New York (WBASNY) argues against the death penalty in the following viewpoint. The association offers several reasons why the death penalty should be abolished: An error-free death penalty is an impossibility; the death penalty is discriminatory and arbitrary; the death penalty does not deter crime; and the public does not support the death penalty. The Women's Bar Association of the State of New York is an organization of attorneys and judges.

As you read, consider the following questions:

1. What evidence does the WBASNY offer in support of its assertion that capital punishment is racially discriminatory?
2. What evidence does the WBASNY offer to support its claim that the death penalty does not deter crime?
3. What is the impact of life in prison without parole, according to the WBASNY?

Women's Bar Association of the State of New York, State Assembly Hearings, January 21 and 25, 2005.

The Women's Bar Association of the State of New York (WBASNY) welcomes the opportunity to comment on the future of capital punishment in the State of New York. WBASNY, founded in 1980, has a membership of more than 3,200 attorneys across the state, including prosecutors, defense attorneys, public officials, and members of the judiciary. Our mission is to promote the advancement of the status of women in the legal profession; to promote the fair and equal administration of justice; and to act as a unified voice for our members with respect to issues of statewide, national and international significance to women generally and to women attorneys in particular.

Our position, consistent since well before the current issue was raised in 1995, is that there is no place for capital punishment in the State of New York. We believe that justice for all is better served by a sentence of life imprisonment without the availability of parole ("life in prison without parole") than by reinstitution of the death penalty. Families of victims will have a sense of psychological finality and retribution for their loss, while the community at large will be adequately protected. At the same time, the state will have imposed a penalty which is humane and does not beget violence by example.

Consistent with the testimony of our colleague New York bar associations and the position of the American Bar Association and scores of others, we believe that the death penalty is cruel and unusual. We believe that New York, progressive in its approach to fairness and justice in the courts, can and should be a leader in the movement against capital punishment. Our reasons are not exhaustive. Rather, they are intended to raise issues congruent with WBASNY's legislative and policy positions, as follows: It is impossible to design a system of capital punishment that is not subject to error, and that can be fairly and uniformly and impartially administered. The capital punishment system is racially discriminatory and geographically and otherwise arbitrary in its application. Capital punishment does not deter murder. A sentence of life in prison without parole simultaneously serves the criminal justice functions of incarceration, retribution and deterrence while preserving the possibility of future legal proceedings based on scientific procedures and evidence not available at the time of the defendant's trial. Finally, there is growing recognition, across the country and the world, that capital punishment is inherently cruel.

There Is No Error-Free Death Penalty

Since 1973, 117 people have been exonerated and freed from death row across the country, as the result of DNA or other evidence not available at the time of trial. In 2000, in a landmark study of over 4,500 capital appeals from 34 states, the overall rate of reversible error found in capital sentences was 68%. This means that at least 3,060 people sentenced to death at the trial level had errors during the course of their trials serious enough to merit having those sentences overturned. Of those reversed, fully 7% were found not guilty on retrial.

These chilling statistics clearly show that no system is free from mistakes, regardless of the efforts of legislators and the criminal justice system. We note that in crafting the New York statute, the legislature included a number of the 1995 suggestions of our own and other Bar Associations to protect defendants' rights. Nevertheless, we believe that it is not possible for any government to ever craft or administer capital punishment in a way that will ensure that no mistake will ever be made. In our view, the unavoidable possibility that even one innocent person will be executed is simply too great a price to pay.

Racial Discrimination

In this country, studies have shown that race, especially that of the victim, is the prime determinant of whether a person is sentenced to death. Over two decades ago, one study, accepted as statistically valid by the United States Supreme Court, found that those who killed whites were eleven times more likely to receive the death penalty than those who killed blacks. Even when the figures were adjusted to account for other factors that may have contributed to the disparity, it was found that when the victim was white, the perpetrator was still more than four times likely to be sentenced to death.

This unacceptable disparity continues to this day. In 2004, 50% of murder victims in this country were minorities. However, only 12% of those executed were convicted of murdering a member of a minority race—and NO white person was executed for killing an African American.

The perpetrators' own race is also a significant factor in determining whether the government will seek to execute them. According to the US Department of Justice, 70% of those recommended for the death penalty in the federal system are minorities. Of those eventually sentenced to death, 80% are minorities.

Call an Immediate Halt to Executions

The United States government and the state governments should call an immediate halt to executions. Capital punishment has been abolished by most modern industrialized nations, it is not a deterrent to murder, and its administration in the United States is replete with error, injustice, and discrimination.

Phoebe C. Ellsworth, Craig Haney, and Mark Costanzo, "Position Statement on the Death Penalty," Society for the Psychology Study of Social Issues, February 9, 2001. www.spssi.org.

While the numbers in this state are not as dramatic, unfortunately the same principles apply. Between 1995 and 2003, only 30% of First Degree Murder indictments in New York involved a white victim. However, 48% of all cases in which the District Attorney chose to file a death notice involved a white victim. In the first eight years since the death penalty was re-introduced in New York, 60% of all cases in which the District Attorney filed a death notice involved defendants of a minority race.

The Death Penalty Is Geographically Arbitrary

In New York, although upstate counties (the 53 counties north of Westchester) experience only 20% of all homicides, they nonetheless account for 65% of all capital prosecutions. Moreover, just six of New York's 62 counties account for 56% of all death notices filed in the state.

A similar geographic arbitrariness is apparent nationwide. Nationally, one region of the country—the South—accounts for 85% of all executions in the country, despite the fact that it has nowhere near 85% of the population or even 85% of all murders.

Reasonable minds may differ on the efficacy or appropriateness of capital punishment. Surely, however, all can agree that whether one lives or dies for one's crime should not be determined by the color of one's skin or the place the crime happened to have occurred.

The Death Penalty Does Not Deter Crime

Statistics gathered by the FBI confirm that the death penalty is not a deterrent to murder. For example, the South, which has executed 776 people since 1976, had the highest murder rate in the country in 2001, 2002 and 2003, and was the only region with an above-average homicide rate in each of those years. By contrast, the Northeast, which has seen 3 executions since 1976, had the lowest murder rate in each of those years and was the only region with a below-average rate. And these three years are not an anomaly. The average homicide rate for non-death penalty states is and has always been lower than the average homicide rate for states with the death penalty. A September 2000 *New York Times* survey of FBI statistics to that date showed that over the previous twenty years, the homicide rate in states with the death penalty was 48%–101% higher than in states without the death penalty.

In January of 2000, former Attorney General Janet Reno stated in a weekly Justice Department News Briefing, "I have inquired for most of my adult life about studies that might show that the death penalty is a deterrent. And I have not seen any research that would substantiate that point." It is time for New York to recognize what the Attorney General of the United States did five years ago: capital punishment does not stop or even lessen murder.

Life in Prison

A sentence of life in prison without parole simultaneously serves the criminal justice functions of incarceration, retribution and deterrence while preserving the possibility of future legal proceedings based on scientific procedures and evidence not available at the time of the defendant's trial, and perhaps even release of those wrongfully convicted.

At the same time, we believe that the severity of life in prison without parole merits the continuing provision of state funded services to the accused as currently provided by the Capital Defenders Office. We therefore would strongly urge that abolition of the death penalty should not be a justification for cutting the budget of an office that ensures that the rights of minorities and the indigent are protected.

The Inherent Flaws

In 1995, there was a great deal of support in this state and country for the death penalty. As more and more of the problems discussed above have come to light, there has been a marked shift in public opinion.

One indicator of public support, or lack thereof, for capital punishment is the imposition of the sentence. Since 1999, death sentences have decreased by 54%, executions are down 40% and the population on death row has dropped by 4%. Further, Gallup Polls over the past five years have recorded a steady decline in public support for capital punishment.

Illinois famously declared a moratorium on capital prosecution in 2000. All capital cases in New Jersey have been put on hold due to questions about methods of execution. California, the state with the largest death row population, has commissioned a study of the death penalty to uncover risks and flaws in the system. The American Bar Association, the New York State Bar Association, the New York County Lawyers Association, the Association of the Bar of the City of New York, and dozens of other local and statewide bar associations across the land have all called for a moratorium on executions in their respective jurisdictions. Numerous governmental entities have passed similar resolutions.

Internationally, over half the countries of the world have abolished capital punishment. Indeed, 26 countries have done so since New York re-instated it in 1995.

It is clear that an ever-increasing population of both this country and the world recognizes that capital punishment, no matter how it is administered, is always cruel, inhuman and degrading. As Manhattan District Attorney Robert Morgenthau eloquently testified at the December 15, 2004 session of the Joint Assembly Hearings on the Death Penalty in New York:

Some crimes are so depraved that execution might seem a

just penalty. But even in the virtually impossible event that a statute could be crafted and applied so wisely that it would reach only those cases, the price would be too high. When the state kills, it sends the wrong message. The death penalty is an endorsement of violent solutions, and violence begets violence.

It is for all of these reasons that the Women's Bar Association of the State of New York remains opposed to any legislation that would reinstate the death penalty in New York.

> "For some crimes, [the death penalty] represents the only just punishment available on earth."

The Death Penalty Must Be Maintained

Dudley Sharp

In the following viewpoint Dudley Sharp contends that the death penalty is necessary and should be maintained. He asserts that the death penalty is the most appropriate form of punishment for vile crimes such as murder. Further, he argues that there is no proof that even one innocent person has been executed. He also asserts that the death penalty saves innocent lives and argues that most Americans support the death penalty. Dudley Sharp is the vice president of Justice for All, a criminal justice reform organization.

As you read, consider the following questions:
1. Who were Jenny Ertman and Elizabeth Peûa, as reported by the author?
2. What is Sharp's response to the Death Penalty Information Center's assertion that many innocent people have been executed?
3. How does the death penalty save lives, according to Sharp?

Dudley Sharp, "Do We Need the Death Penalty? Yes, It's Still Necessary," *The World & I Online*, September 2002. Copyright © 2002 by News World Communications, Inc. Reproduced by permission.

There is nothing quite like hanging out with your best friend. Jenny Ertman, 14, and Elizabeth Peûa, 16, shared their hopes and dreams with each other. Like millions of other teenagers, they liked to have fun, to laugh and smile. One summer evening in Houston, Texas, they shared their last moments on earth together—their own murders.

They were late returning home and took a shortcut through the woods, next to some railroad tracks. They ran into a gang initiation. They were both raped: orally, anally, and vaginally. The gang members laughed about the virgin blood they spilled. When they had finished, they beat and strangled the girls. But Jenny and Elizabeth wouldn't die. With all their strength, with their souls still holding on to the beautiful lives before them, they fought for life.

The gang worked harder. The girls were strangled with belts and shoelaces, stomped on and beaten. Their dreams disappeared as life seeped away from their broken bodies.

Their parents are left to visit empty rooms, to cry upon the beds of their daughters and think what could have been. How beautiful Elizabeth would have been in her prom dress. Her corsage was replaced by the flowers on her grave. And Jenny's future children, would their grandparents have spoiled them? You know the answer. The immutable joy of grandchildren's laughter was silenced by the cruel selfishness of murder.

Justice Determines the Punishment

Sometimes, the death penalty is simply the most appropriate punishment for the vile crime committed. In such cases, jurors are given the choice between a death sentence and a variety of life sentences, depending upon the jurisdiction. It is never easy for juries to give a death sentence. Neither hatred nor revenge is part of their deliberations. The search for justice determines the punishment.

The murder of the innocent is undeserved. The punishment of murderers has been earned by the pain and suffering they have imposed on their victims. Execution cannot truly represent justice, because there is no recompense to balance the weight of murder. For some crimes, it represents the only just punishment available on earth.

Today, much more than justice is part of the death penalty discussion. Opponents are relentlessly attacking the penalty process itself. They insist that it is so fraught with error and caprice that it should be abandoned. At the very least, they say, America should impose a national moratorium so the system can be reviewed.

Fraudulent Innocence Statistics

The leading salvo in those claims is that 101 innocent people have been released from death row with evidence of their innocence. The number is a fraud. Unfortunately, both the international media and, most predictably, the U.S. media have swallowed such claims and passed them along to the public. Even many of our elected officials in Washington have blindly accepted those numbers. Sen. Patrick Leahy, chairman of the Senate Judiciary Committee, has said: "What we know is that nearly 100 innocent people have been released from death row since 1973."

The source for these claims is the Death Penalty Information Center (DPIC), the leading source of antideath penalty material in the United States. Richard Dieter, head of the DPIC, has admitted, in the June 6, 2000, *ABA Journal*, that his group makes no distinction between the legally innocent ("I got off death row because of legal error") and the actually innocent ("I had no connection to the murder") cases. Although the DPIC has attempted to revise its standards for establishing innocence, none of the various contortions even suggests actual innocence.

As everyone knows, the debate is about the actually innocent. To strengthen their case, death penalty opponents have broadened their "innocent" count by cases that don't merit that description. On June 20 [2002], for example, the Florida Commission on Capital Cases released its review of 23 death sentence cases that the DPIC had called into question. Its conclusion was that in only 4 of those cases were there doubts as to guilt.

Though the DPIC claims that 101 cases were released from death row with evidence of innocence, the actual number is closer to 30. That is 30 cases out of 7,000 sentenced to death since 1973. It appears that the death penalty may well be this country's most accurate criminal sanction, when taking into account the percentage of actual innocents convicted (0.4 percent) and the thoroughness of preventing those allegedly innocent from being executed (100 percent).

Are You in Favor of the Death Penalty for a Person Convicted of Murder?

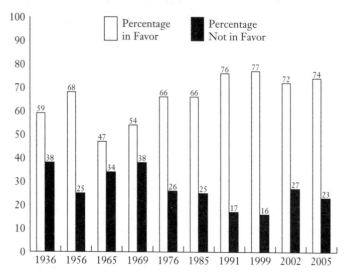

Statistics from Jeffrey M. Jones, "Americans' Views of Death Penalty More Positive This Year," Gallup Organization, May 19, 2005.

Of all the world's social and governmental institutions that put innocents at risk, I can find only one, the U.S. death penalty, that has no proof of an innocent killed since 1900. Can you think of another?

Saving Innocent Lives

Two other factors weigh into the innocence consideration. First, the death penalty remains the most secure form of incapacitation, meaning that executed murderers do not harm and murder again. Living murderers do, quite often. This is unchallenged. Second, although the deterrent effect of capital punishment has been unjustifiably maligned, the evidence is overwhelming that the potential for negative consequences deters or alters behavior. History and the social sciences fully support that finding.

Three major studies were released in 2001, all finding for the deterrent effect of the death penalty. One, out of Emory University, finds that "each execution results, on average, in 18 fewer murders—with a margin of error of plus or minus 10."

Another, out of the University of Houston, found that a temporary halt to executions in Texas resulted in an additional 90–150 murders, because of the reduction in deterrence. One author, Professor C. Robert Cloninger, states: "[Our] recent study is but another of a growing list of empirical work that finds evidence consistent with the deterrent hypothesis. It is the cumulative effect of these studies that causes any neutral observer to pause." Death penalty opponents want us to believe that the most severe criminal sanction—execution—deters no one. However, if reason is your guide and you remain unsure of deterrence, you are left with the following consideration. If the death penalty does deter, halting executions will cause more innocents to be slaughtered by giving murderers an additional opportunity to harm and murder again. If the death penalty does not deter, executions will punish murderers as the jury deems appropriate, preventing them from harming any more victims. Clearly, ending or reducing executions will put many more innocents at risk.

Another major factor in the debate was introduced in a study headed by James Liebman, a professor at Columbia University Law School. A Broken System: Error Rates in Capital Cases revealed that there was a 68 percent reversal rate in death penalty cases from 1973 to 1995. The error rate within that study has not been publicly discussed.

Faulty Data

Professors Barry Latzer and James Cauthen of John Jay College of Criminal Justice found a 25 percent error within the study's calculations, bringing the reversal rate down to 52 percent. Unfortunately, they had to accept the accuracy of Liebman's assessments, because he refused to release his database. Case reviews in Florida, New Jersey, Utah, and Nevada have provided specific cause to challenge his data. Florida challenges any assessment of error in 33 percent of the cases identified by Liebman, suggesting that the national "error" rate may be closer to 35 percent.

But even that number is suspect. The Supreme Court has stated that the death penalty system receives super due process. This means that the courts are extraordinarily generous in granting reversals in death penalty cases. In fact, the appellate courts are twice as likely to reverse the sentence in death penalty cases as they are the conviction.

Racial and Economic Bias Has Been Debunked

Traditionally, death penalty opponents have stated that racism and poverty determine who receives the death penalty. Those arguments persist. What they fail to reveal is that white murderers are twice as likely to be executed as black murderers and are executed 12 months faster.

Some claim that the race of the victim determines the sentence. While those who murder whites dominate death row, it is also true that, overwhelmingly, whites are the victims in robberies, rapes, burglaries, and carjackings, which make up the majority of death penalty crimes.

No one disputes that the wealthy have an advantage in avoiding a death sentence. The United States executes about 0.1 percent of its murderers. Is there any evidence that it is less likely to execute the wealthier ones, based on the ratio of wealthier to poorer capital murderers? Surprisingly, no.

The Value of Life

This brings me back to where I started: justice. Some say that executions show a contempt for human life, but the opposite is true. We would hope that a brutal rape may result in a life sentence. Why? We value freedom so highly that we take freedom away as punishment. If freedom were not valued, taking it away would be no sanction.

Life is considered even more precious. Therefore, the death penalty is considered the severest sanction for the most horrible of crimes. Even murderers tell us that they value life (their own) more than freedom. That is why over 99 percent of convicted capital murderers seek a life sentence, not a death sentence, during the punishment phase of their trials.

Even some of those traditionally against capital punishment have decided that some crimes are justly punished with death. Timothy McVeigh's 2001 execution was thought a just punishment by 81 percent of the American people, reflecting an all-time high of support. When 168 innocents were murdered, including 19 children whom McVeigh described as "collateral damage," the collective conscience of the American people reached an overwhelming consensus. A Gallup poll, released on May 20 [2002], shows that 72 percent supported the death penalty, with nearly half those polled saying the sanction is not imposed enough.

Justice for the Innocents

Why didn't I invoke the murder of 3,100 innocents on September 11? Because the murder of one Jenny Ertman is enough—much too much. Which one of the murdered innocents was more valuable than another? Was one child blown apart in Oklahoma City not enough? Was a father forever lost on September 11 not enough? A son? A granddaughter?

Is it the numbers, at all? No, it is the realization that those innocent lives, so willfully ripped from us, represent individuals who contributed to someone's life and happiness. The sheer numbers of murders committed each year may numb us beyond what an individual murder can. But that is only because we must shield ourselves from the absolute horror represented by one innocent murdered. It is a matter of emotional self-preservation.

Often, in the most horrible of times, we find that the goodness in people stands out. At one point during the attack, Jenny was able to escape and run away. Elizabeth's cries brought Jenny back in a fruitless attempt to aid her friend. Love, friendship, and devotion overcame fear.

Of the six attackers who brutalized these girls for over an hour, five received the death penalty. The sixth was too young to prosecute for death. And why did five separate juries give death? Justice.

"*In order for the death penalty to remain a meaningful and effective punishment . . . legislators and judges need to make necessary changes.*"

The Death Penalty Must Be Reformed

Steven D. Stewart

In the following viewpoint Steven D. Stewart contends that although the death penalty is flawed, it is a necessary part of American justice and ought to be reformed rather than abolished. The death penalty is the only way to make sure a murderer never murders again, he points out. Although Stewart grants that some mistakes are inevitable, he also contends that the many safeguards in place for death penalty cases prevent unfair sentencing. Because he sees the death penalty as vitally important to the criminal justice system, Stewart urges legislators and judges to make sure appropriate changes to the death penalty are made. Steven D. Stewart is the prosecuting attorney for Clark County, Indiana.

As you read, consider the following questions:
1. In Stewart's opinion, what problems with the death penalty currently exist?
2. How many inmates released from death row does Stewart term "factually innocent"?
3. What analogy does Stewart draw between the death penalty and an automobile accident?

Steven D. Stewart, "A Message from the Prosecuting Attorney," www.clark prosecutor.org, 2004.

A long with almost three-fourths of the American public, I believe in capital punishment. I believe that there are some defendants who have earned the ultimate punishment our society has to offer by committing murder with aggravating circumstances present. I believe life is sacred. It cheapens the life of an innocent murder victim to say that society has no right to keep the murderer from ever killing again. In my view, society has not only the right, but the duty to act in self defense to protect the innocent.

Death Penalty Shortcomings

Nevertheless, the value of the death penalty in our current system of justice is a limited one and should not be overstated. Because the death sentence is so rarely carried out, whatever deterrent value that exists is lessened in years of appeals and due process. Because of the unlimited power of Governors, judges, juries, and prosecutors to show mercy, the difference between those who receive the death penalty and those who do not is minimal. Finally, because the system allows it, the financial costs to state and local governments can be staggering.

The Right Thing to Do

In spite of these shortcomings, it is my view that pursuing a death sentence in appropriate cases is the right thing to do. There is no adequate and acceptable alternative. Life Without Parole does not eliminate the risk that the prisoner will murder a guard, a visitor, or another inmate, and we should not be compelled to take that risk. It is also not unheard of for inmates to escape from prison. The prisoner will not be eligible for parole until the next legislative session, when the parole laws can be changed. Considering that a defendant sentenced to "life imprisonment" across the country actually serves on the average less than 8 years in prison, it is a good bet that "life without parole" will not have the meaning intended as years go by. Even the most "law and order" legislators will begin to consider alternatives when the medical bills for geriatric care of prisoners start rolling in.

No system of justice can produce results which are 100% certain all the time. Mistakes will be made in any system which relies upon human testimony for proof. We should be vigilant to uncover and avoid such mistakes. Our system of justice rightfully demands a higher standard for death penalty cases. However, the risk of making a mistake with the extraordinary due process applied in death penalty cases is very small, and there is no credible evidence to show that any innocent persons have been executed at least since the death penalty was reactivated in 1976. The 100+ death row inmates "innocent", "exonerated" and released, as trumpeted by anti–death penalty activists, is a fraud. The actual number of factually innocent released death row inmates is closer to 40, and in any event should be considered in context of over 7,000 death sentences handed down since 1973. It stands as the most accurate judgment/sentence in any system of justice ever created. The inevitability of a mistake should not serve as grounds to eliminate the death penalty any more than the risk of having a fatal wreck should make automobiles illegal. At the same time, we should never ignore the risks of allowing the inmate to kill again.

Necessary Changes

Our "system" was created by legislators and judges. In order for the death penalty to remain a meaningful and effective punishment, those same legislators and judges need to make necessary changes to reflect the will of the people in a democratic society.

"[We] should . . . work to abolish an irrevocable punishment that is too flawed to fix."

The Death Penalty Is Too Flawed to Be Fixed

Amnesty International

In the following viewpoint Amnesty International argues that there are irreparable flaws in the way that death penalty cases are handled. The organization summarizes the cases of several death row inmates who were exonerated because of errors in their trials, demonstrating the problems with the death penalty. It contends that the death penalty is too flawed to fix and urges that it be abolished. Amnesty International is an international organization whose mission is to address human rights issues around the world.

As you read, consider the following questions:
1. Why did Illinois governor George Ryan call for a moratorium on the death penalty in his state, according to Amnesty International?
2. As stated by the author, what did the Commission on Capital Punishment report?
3. Who are Christopher Simmons and Aaron Patterson, according to the author?

On 31 January 2000, Governor George Ryan of Illinois took a courageous step. He announced a moratorium on executions in his state because of its "shameful record of convicting innocent people and putting them on death row". The cases of 13 such people had come to light in Illinois since 1987. They included Anthony Porter, whose wrongful conviction was uncovered, not by the system, but by a group of students who happened to take up his case as a university project. Anthony Porter was released in 1999 after more than 16 years on death row for a crime he did not commit. He had come within 48 hours of execution in 1998.

The Illinois Commission's Report

On 15 April 2002, the 14-member Commission on Capital Punishment appointed by Governor Ryan in March 2000 to review the death penalty system in Illinois published its report. It is a thorough publication, which makes 85 recommendations for reform, ranging from videotaping police interrogations, to placing local prosecutors' decisions to seek the death penalty under state-level review, to reducing the number of crimes punishable by death. In its preamble to the report, the Commission explains: "Because capital punishment is presently lawful in Illinois and because it appears to have the support of a majority of Illinois citizens, our deliberations have concentrated primarily on these reforms and other proposals, rather than on the merits of capital punishment."

"Only at the close of our work did we consider that question", the preamble continues, and goes on to reveal that a "majority of the Commission would favor that the death penalty be abolished in Illinois." The report concludes with similar food for thought: "The Commission was unanimous in the belief that no system, given human nature and frailties, could ever be devised or constructed that would work perfectly and guarantee absolutely that no innocent person is ever again sentenced to death."

Amnesty International's Recommendations

On 15 April, Governor Ryan accepted the Commission's report and called on the Illinois legislature to act on its proposals. The Governor has already said that he will review the

The Death Penalty Experiment Has Failed

From this day forward, I no longer shall tinker with the machinery of death. For more than twenty years I have endeavored—indeed, I have struggled—along with a majority of this Court, to develop procedural and substantive rules that would lend more than the mere appearance of fairness to the death penalty endeavor. Rather than continue to coddle the Court's delusion that the desired level of fairness has been achieved and the need for regulation eviscerated, I feel morally and intellectually obligated simply to concede that the death penalty experiment has failed. It is virtually self-evident to me now that no combination of procedural rules or substantive regulations ever can save the death penalty from its inherent constitutional deficiencies. The basic question—does the system accurately and consistently determine which defendants "deserve" to die?—cannot be answered in the affirmative. It is not simply that this Court has allowed vague aggravating circumstances to be employed, . . . relevant mitigating evidence to be disregarded, . . . and vital judicial review to be blocked. . . . The problem is that the inevitability of factual, legal, and moral error gives us a system that we know must wrongly kill some defendants, a system that fails to deliver the fair, consistent, and reliable sentences of death required by the Constitution.

Justice Harry Blackmun, dissenting opinion, *Callins v. Collins*, February 22, 1994.

---

cases of all those on death row in the state (currently 161 people) before he leaves office in January 2003.[1] Amnesty International believes that the best way for him to continue what he started two years ago would be to commute all of these death sentences. His moratorium decision has had a profound impact beyond the borders of Illinois, causing people and politicians around the United States to question the fairness and reliability of a system in which there has all too often been something approaching blind faith. It was a decision that showed the sort of leadership that has been sadly lacking in a country that finds itself on the wrong side of history on the death penalty.

Meanwhile, the Illinois legislature should take the Commission's conclusion to heart, and work to abolish an irrevocable punishment that is too flawed to fix.[2] Legislators should

1. Ryan commuted all death sentences on January 11, 2003.   2. Illinois retains the death penalty, but the moratorium continues.

never forget that it was sheer chance that the state did not kill Anthony Porter for a crime he did not commit. They should recognize that the only guarantee against that happening to anyone else in the future is for the state to permanently retire its executioners.

But this is not an issue confined to Illinois. Indeed Anthony Porter is only one of 100 people to be released from the country's death rows since 1973 after evidence of their innocence emerged. Others have been sent to their deaths despite serious doubts about their guilt. The State of Missouri is currently seeking an execution date for Joseph Amrine. All three of his original accusers, on which his conviction rests, now admit that they lied when they testified that Amrine was the murderer. Presented with such evidence, a number of the jurors from the original trial have stated their belief that they convicted the wrong man. In South Carolina, the state intends to kill Richard Johnson on 3 May 2002, despite the fact that another person has confessed to the murder since his trial. A South Carolina Supreme Court justice has said that "to deny Johnson a new trial in the face of a confession by someone who was admittedly present when the murder was committed would constitute a denial of fundamental fairness shocking to the universal sense of justice."

Justice and Decency

The universal sense of justice and decency will be similarly outraged if Christopher Simmons and Aaron Patterson are killed by the state, as they are due to be, in Missouri and Texas on 1 May and 28 August 2002 respectively. Both were 17 at the time of their crimes. The US leads a tiny handful of countries still willing to flout the international legal prohibition on the use of the death penalty for the crimes of children. It also continues to execute the mentally impaired and those afforded inadequate representation, in contravention of international safeguards.[3]

With 10 people already scheduled to be lethally injected in Texas in May and June, this year [2002] will likely see the

3. In June 2002 the U.S. Supreme Court ended execution of those who are mentally impaired. In March 2005 the Court banned juvenile executions.

800th execution in the USA since judicial killing resumed there in 1977. Each person executed was sentenced under a system characterized by arbitrariness and discrimination. Another 3,700 condemned men and women await execution. Each, together with his or her family, is daily subjected to a cruelty that has been abolished in law or practice by 111 countries. The USA's determination to cling to the wreckage of this degrading policy starkly gives the lie to its claim to be a progressive force for human rights.

Governors and legislators in the United States should build on the example set by Governor Ryan on this fundamental human rights issue. They should summon up the courage to lead their respective jurisdictions away from the death penalty and into the modern world.

"Taxpayers . . . have discovered that death penalty trials are incredibly expensive."

The Death Penalty Costs Too Much

George Sjostrom

In the following viewpoint George Sjostrom maintains that the cost of the death penalty is too high, both in dollars and in emotional pain. He cites economic statistics comparing the costs of death penalty and non–death penalty cases, arguing that death penalty cases are much more expensive. In addition, he tallies the emotional costs of a death penalty trial on all those involved, including family, friends, jurors, and the accused. These trials put all involved through incredible emotional pain, he asserts. George Sjostrom is a freelance writer whose column appears biweekly in the *Ventura County Star.*

As you read, consider the following questions:

1. According to Sjostrom, how much does it cost to try someone in a death penalty trial in California?
2. What are the steps in the appeals process, as related by the author?
3. What are some of the emotional costs of a death penalty trial that Sjostrom names?

M ore and more Americans are in growing disagreement with the death penalty system, some out of moral persuasion, but most because they see death penalty sentences as travesties of the judicial process.

In California, since the death penalty was reinstated by the Supreme Court in 1977, over 600 criminals have been given the death penalty, but only 11 of them have been executed. There are so many criminals awaiting the death penalty that California is considering a $220 million annex to San Quentin's death row, just to house them.

A Gallup poll has found that Americans favoring verdicts of life sentence without the possibility of parole over the death penalty are increasing. There are those who cite the moral objection, thou shalt not kill.

The Death Penalty: Inefficient and Expensive

There are those who cite ethical reasons, some innocents have been put to death. There are some who cite logical reasons—there is no evidence that the death penalty acts as a deterrent to violent crime. And then there are the taxpayers, those who have discovered that death penalty trials are incredibly expensive, and incredibly inefficient.

A study of Los Angeles County trials has shown that the average trial in which prosecutors demand the death penalty costs $1,898,323, while a murder trial where the death penalty is not sought comes in at $627,322. Most of the difference is accounted for by legal fees.

Death trials traditionally require a more complicated jury selection process, longer trials, more expert testimony, more motions filed for change of venue and mistrial, and the automatic provision for mandatory appeal.

According to the *Sacramento Bee*, "The death penalty costs California $90 million annually beyond the ordinary costs of the justice system, $78 million of that incurred at the trial level."

The Appeal Process

The appeal process is the most costly part. In a California death penalty case, the following appeal steps are typical, and almost automatic:

- Trial court death sentence is automatically appealed to State Supreme Court.
- Once the State Supreme Court rejects the appeal, defendant asks the U.S. Supreme Court to review the state decision.
- If the federal court finds any error in the proceedings, the trial may be sent back to the state court for review, and the process starts over again.

The Emotional Cost

But whatever the price to the taxpayer, whatever the profit to the attorneys, the ultimate torture is on the families of both the victim and the accused. A death penalty trial puts an almost unbearable emotional burden on those whose loved one has been killed and on those whose loved one is about to be put to death.

Costs of California's Death Penalty

- It costs $90,000 more per year to house an inmate on death row than in the general prison population, for a total of $57.5 million annually.

- The 11 executions over the past 27 years have cost on average $250 million *each*.

- The Attorney General spends about 15% of his criminal division budget, or about $11 million annually on capital cases.

- A capital murder trial costs three times more to try than a non-capital murder trial.

- The Office of the State Public Defender, which represents some death row inmates, has a budget of $11.3 million annually.

- The Habeas Corpus Resource Center represents inmates and trains death penalty attorneys on a budget of $11 million annually.

- Federal public defenders and appointed attorneys receive $12 million annually.

Rone Tempest, *Los Angeles Times*, March 6, 2005.

In capital cases, the jury is put through what amounts to a second trial, to reaffirm their already-arrived-at decision of death. Mother, father, family and friends testify in front of

the penalty jury about how much they loved and missed t
victim. Parents, siblings and friends testify about what
good guy the convicted felon really is.

This is an emotional purgatory that comes only with the
death penalty. And then there are the jurists, left with the
gruesome burden of conscience that they have done what
most of us couldn't bear, to put another human to death.

In the Scott Peterson[1] trial, after months of deliberations
resulting in a guilty verdict, the jury had to listen to another
seven days of tearful pleas, followed by three more days of
deliberation, to affirm their death penalty verdict.

Thirteen of our states have no death penalty. Among the
37 states that have capital punishment, California has more
"death eligible" crimes than any other state. We also have
the largest condemned-to-death population in the nation.

It's time for California to reconsider its death penalty. We
are torturing families, friends, relatives, taxpayers and jurors
while the heinous criminal sits in the first row, in seeming
enjoyment of his circus of attention.

---

1. Peterson was sentenced to death on March 17, 2005, for the murder of his preg-
nant wife.

"The available evidence . . . suggests that capital punishment, if carried out with any degree of regularity, can be cost effective."

The Death Penalty Does Not Cost Too Much

Jon Sorensen

Jon Sorenson contends in the following viewpoint that the cost of the death penalty is not too high. He argues that high cost estimates by death penalty opponents are based on questionable math. He also notes that changes in state laws redefining life sentencing will add considerably to the cost of maintaining a prisoner. Given that capital punishment has become more efficient, its costs have been reduced and are actually less than life imprisonment.

As you read, consider the following questions:
1. How much does a death penalty case cost in Texas, according to the *Dallas Morning News*, and what is the real figure, according to Sorensen?
2. What are some of the items Sorensen says are used in calculating the cost of capital punishment?
3. How much longer will an inmate spend in North Carolina prisons serving a life sentence under the new law, in the author's view?

Jon Sorensen, "The Administration of Capital Punishment," *ACJS Today*, vol. 29, May/June 2004, pp. 1, 4–5, 7. Copyright © 2005 by the Academy of Criminal Justice Sciences. Reproduced by permission.

P rior to the modern era, the cost of capital punishment was not really an issue for the sanction was carried out relatively quickly and efficiently. However, the "super due process" afforded capital defendants in the modern era has meant extensive appeals, numerous reversals, and associated delays in the execution of death sentences. A series of studies conducted mainly by journalists since the late 1980s have found the procedures associated with the death penalty to be quite costly, exceeding by far the cost of life imprisonment. Again the most prolific disseminator of these findings has been the DPIC [Death Penalty Information Center], stating that the overall cost of the death penalty is about $2 to $3 million per execution. Because these estimates are based on questionable assumptions, however, they should not be uncritically accepted.

Questionable Assumptions

One of the studies quoted extensively in the popular press, on websites, and in the academic literature was published by the *Dallas Morning News*, which estimated the cost of a death penalty case in Texas to be $2.3 million. Many of the specific cost estimates used in the study appear to be well-grounded and are consistent with other available sources. For instance, the reporter estimated the cost of a death penalty trial to be $266k, the cost of state and federal appeals to amount to nearly $200k, and the cost of incarceration on death row prior to execution to be $137k. However, the reporter included a mysterious $1.7 million "estimate of appellate court costs and outlays associated with the death penalty." Excluding this unfathomable and completely unverifiable "per capita" estimate, a death penalty case in Texas, at about $600k, would appear to fare favorably with a "40-year" life sentence, which was estimated to cost $750k in the same report.

The Example of North Carolina

While the *Dallas Morning News* report and those completed by other journalists provide only rough estimates, economists have occasionally been enlisted to study the issue. The first comprehensive examination was performed by Duke researchers to estimate the cost of capital punishment in North Carolina. [Philip] Cook and colleagues included in their calculations not only the direct costs of litigation, such as fees for public defenders, prosecutors, and judges, but they also calculated an hourly "load" rate that would account for the indirect costs associated with trial, as well as appeals and retrials. The researchers performed similar calculations for non-capital trials where defendants were sentenced to a 20-year "life" prison sentence. They provided two separate cost estimates. In the first, a capital murder case was found to exceed the cost of a non-capital first-degree murder case by $163k ($67k over the cost of a non-capital trial plus an additional $262k for appeals, minus $166k in prison savings). In a second estimate, the researchers calculated the cost for "successful" capital prosecutions, meaning those resulting in execution, including the costs associated with reversals, resentencing, and ultimately housing for life many of those initially sentenced to death. Assuming a 10% successful execution rate for those initially prosecuted as capital murder, the cost per execution was estimated to be $2.16 million. While this is the figure favored by the DPIC [Death Penalty Information Center] and other abolitionist groups, the researchers admit that the estimate is tenuous and dramatically affected by the percentage of death penalty cases assumed to result in executions. For example, the authors' calculation of cost savings per execution decreases to $780k if the hypothetical execution rate is increased to 30%.

A Change in the Law Changes Costs

Their study, however, was completed in 1993, before a major change in the statutory definition of "life." Rather than

20 years, North Carolina inmates convicted of capital murder must now serve the rest of their natural life in prison with no possibility for parole. Given the average age at entrance to prison and the average life expectancy, it has been estimated that such inmates will serve about 47 years behind bars. Including the additional 27 years of confinement, the total cost of a life sentence would be $593k. Under the current definition of life, the cost associated with a capital murder case in North Carolina appears to be a bargain, saving the state $264k in incarceration costs. Also in recent years, the percentage of death penalty cases resulting in executions has increased dramatically from the early modern era, lowering the costs associated with unsuccessful capital murder prosecutions. Given the lack of parole eligibility, the cost savings of life imprisonment essentially washes out when the rate of success in executing death sentences reaches 50%.

The available evidence thus suggests that capital punishment, if carried out with any degree of regularity, can be cost effective. . . .

The process itself has become more efficient without sacrificing protection for defendants. Capital punishment in *active* death penalty jurisdictions is at least as efficient as life imprisonment, and perhaps more so.

"*It would be a cruel way to die: awake, paralysed, unable to move, to breathe, while potassium burned through your veins.*"

Lethal Injection Should Be Abolished

Lancet

The editors of the *Lancet* argue in the following viewpoint that lethal injection is a cruel and inhumane procedure. The editors cite a recent study claiming that those being executed may not be fully anesthetized before the lethal injection is administered. The *Lancet* editors also argue that doctors should not participate in executions because it conflicts with their duty to do no harm. The *Lancet* is a British medical journal.

As you read, consider the following questions:
1. What three drugs are administered during an execution by lethal injection, according to the editors?
2. What do American Medical Association guidelines say about physician participation in executions, according to the *Lancet* editors?
3. What reasons do the editors offer for the abolishment of capital punishment in any form?

L ethal injection is the most common way people are legally put to death in the USA. To be exact, this method has been used to kill 788 of the 956 men and women who have been executed in the USA since 1976, when the death penalty was reinstated by the Supreme Court. Lethal injection is supposed to be humane, and thus not in violation of the US Constitution's Eighth Amendment proscription against "cruel and unusual" punishment. Indeed, compared with electrocution, gas, gunfire, or hanging, killing people with drugs seems almost humane.

The Details of Lethal Injection

Typically, the condemned man or woman is strapped to a chair or trolley. Two intravenous lines are inserted, one as a back up. The lines are kept open with saline solution. Then, at the warden's signal, the injection team administers: first, sodium thiopental to induce anaesthesia, then pancuronium bromide to cause paralysis, and finally a bolus [intravenous dose] of potassium chloride to bring about cardiac arrest. It seems so clinical and clean.

However, in a fast-track Research Letter in this week's [April 2005] *Lancet*, Leonidas Koniaris and co-workers report that these killings may not be as free from cruelty as death-penalty proponents claim. The research team obtained information from Virginia and Texas, where since 1976 nearly half of the executions in the USA have been done. Among the facts they learned were that neither state has a record of how they developed their execution protocol, that the injection teams were made up of medical technicians or individuals from medical corps with no training in administering anaesthesia, and that there was no assessment of the depth of anaesthesia before the paralysing agent and potassium chloride were injected.

They May Have Been Awake

The researchers also obtained toxicological reports from four other states which indicate that post-mortem thiopental concentrations in the blood of 43 of 49 executed inmates (88%) were lower than those needed for surgical anaesthesia, and 21 (43%) episodes were consistent with awareness. That is: those being executed may have been awake. Of course, because they were paralysed, no one could tell. It would be a cruel way to die: awake, paralysed, unable to move, to breathe, while potassium burned through your veins. That is why, as Koniaris and his co-authors point out, the American Veterinary Medical Association and 19 states, including Texas, prohibit the use of neuromuscular blocking agents to kill animals.

Kauffmann. Copyright © by Joel Kauffmann. Reproduced by permission.

The authors call for a halt to executions by lethal injection and a public review. They also argue that because "participation of doctors in protocol design and execution is ethically prohibited", a more effective, humane protocol cannot be developed. But, ethically prohibited or not, many doctors are willing to participate in putting people to death. A survey of US physicians found that although the American Medical Association (AMA) ethical guidelines forbid physicians to participate in executions, 19% said they would inject lethal drugs and 41% said they would perform at least one action prohibited by the AMA guidelines, such as starting intravenous lines. In fact, only 3% of those asked were aware that there were guidelines.

Doctors Should Not Kill

Clearly, for a substantial number of physicians, the putting to death of condemned people is not considered contrary to the precept "first, do no harm". What justification can there be for capital punishment at all? The two main arguments for the death penalty are deterrence and retribution. Few experts believe that the threat of capital punishment is an effective deterrent. That leaves retribution. But to justify capital punishment, the retribution must be meted out fairly, and that is clearly not the case. In only 1% of murders do prosecutors seek the death penalty. Whether you receive the death penalty depends not on what you have done, but where you committed your crime, what colour your skin is, and how much money you have. The use of the death penalty not only varies from state to state (12 US states have no death penalty) but from jurisdiction to jurisdiction within a state. Repeated studies have shown a pattern of racial discrimination in the administration of the death penalty. Of the 205 people executed for inter-racial murders in the USA, for example, 193 were black defendants charged with killing a white person, while only 12 were white defendants charged with killing a black individual. 90% of defendants are too poor to hire their own lawyer—most rely on overworked court-appointed lawyers.

Capital punishment is not only an atrocity, but also a stain on the record of the world's most powerful democracy. Doctors should not be in the job of killing. Those who do participate in this barbaric act are shameful examples of how a profession has allowed its values to be corrupted by state violence.

"*As any other anesthesiologist will tell you, [the] argument involving [lethal injection] is bogus.*"

Lethal Injection Should Be Maintained

Kyle Janek

In the following viewpoint Kyle Janek asserts that the drugs used in lethal injections provide a pain-free execution. He acknowledges that the American Veterinary Association bars the use of one of the drugs for awake animals, but he notes that prisoners are heavily anaesthetized before they receive this drug. He concludes that objections to lethal injection have neither logic nor science behind them. Kyle Janek is a Texas state senator and an anesthesiologist.

As you read, consider the following questions:

1. According to Janek, what claims are death penalty abolitionists making about the drug pancuronium bromide?
2. What effect does pancuronium bromide have on the body, according to Janek?
3. Why is sodium pentothal administered during an execution, according to Janek?

Kyle Janek, "Attack on Texas' Legal Injections Is Bogus," www.prodeathpenalty.org, February 1, 2004.

"These hardened criminals never again will murder, rape or deal drugs. As governor, I made sure they received the ultimate punishment—death—and Texas is a safer place for it."

—Former Gov. Mark White

For the reason succinctly stated above, the vast majority of Texans support the death penalty.

In fact, the most recent survey on the subject—a Scripps Howard Texas poll conducted last year—found that 76% of Texans support capital punishment. With one notable dip to 42% in 1966, such a high level of public support generally has held true over the last 50 years.

Having no hope of overturning capital punishment itself at the ballot box or through the court system, a few vocal death penalty opponents, including inmates, have rolled out a new strategy to change how it is carried out.

In what amounts to practicing medicine without a license, those critics have started to attack the inclusion of pancuronium bromide as one of the medications used in the lethal injection process. They claim its use is "cruel and unusual."

Is pancuronium bromide some new, untested drug whose sole purpose is to torture? Is it perhaps an exotic street drug that should be outlawed?

Well, actually . . . no.

Looking at the Science

Pancuronium bromide is a federally approved medication used routinely in hundreds of thousands of medical procedures in this country every year. I know that because, as a licensed, practicing anesthesiologist for the last 20 years, I have given pancuronium bromide and similar drugs to thousands of patients in the operating room, albeit with different results.

As any other anesthesiologist will tell you, this argument involving pancuronium bromide is bogus. But for the sake of argument, let's look at the science.

The Texas Department of Criminal Justice uses 3 drugs in its administration of the death penalty: sodium pentothal, pancuronium bromide and potassium chloride.

Sodium pentothal is a barbiturate that until about 10 years ago was the most widely used medication for inducing general anesthesia. (It has since been displaced somewhat by newer drugs that cause fewer side effects upon awakening. For obvious reasons, that isn't a concern for death penalty cases.)

Approval of Lethal Injection to Execute Prisoners

Which comes closer to your view—states should be allowed to execute prisoners sentenced to the death penalty by means of lethal injection, or lethal injection of death row prisoners represents cruel and unusual punishment that should not be permitted?

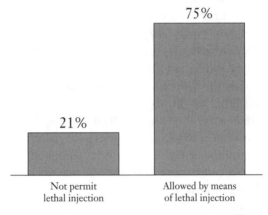

Dennis Welch, Gallup Organization, May 18, 2004. www.gallup.com.

It is important to understand that sodium pentothal is given to an inmate first to render him completely unconscious and insensible to pain. For example, a normal surgical dose for a man weighing 220 pounds would be about 300 milligrams. Yet for lethal injection, the inmate receives 3 grams—or 10 times the normal amount based on body weight. I can attest with all medical certainty that anyone receiving that massive dose will be under anesthesia.

The second of the three drugs given in a lethal injection is pancuronium bromide—the subject of so much recent scrutiny. Pancuronium bromide and its newer cousins are members of a class called neuromuscular blockers. Simply put, those drugs paralyze the body's skeletal muscles. In a lethal injection, the effect of the drug is to relax the chest wall muscles and the diaphragm in the now unconscious inmate.

Euthanasia Guidelines

Now, as has been noted elsewhere, the American Veterinary Medical Association has adopted guidelines for euthanasia that preclude the use of this drug—when it is the only medication given. In other words, it shouldn't be used in animals that are awake.

Some critics recently opined against using pancuronium bromide as part of lethal injection, noting that the state bans its use in animal shelters "because of its potential to shield pain and suffering."

Actually, state law makes no mention of the drug. Rather, it specifically names pentobarbital and compressed carbon monoxide as the drugs that must be used. That was to address some abuses brought forth by animal rights groups that had nothing to do with pancuronium bromide.

The last chemical in the three-drug lethal injection formula is potassium chloride, whose immediate effect in the dose given is to stop the heart and hasten death. In large doses given rapidly to a patient who is awake, the medication would cause pain in the arm due to irritation of the veins through which it courses. But for the sake of emphasis, we aren't talking here about a patient who is awake or even remotely conscious at this point.

The current argument against executions seems to hinge on the supposition that the second and 3rd drugs in this regimen would be cruel to someone who could feel them—and, to be candid, that assertion is true, since the pancuronium would cause a patient to be paralyzed and unable to respond to the pain of the potassium injection.

Yet for that argument to be valid in any way, you must ignore the first drug in the process—sodium pentothal—that (1) renders the inmate to be completely unconscious, (2) has been used for decades to induce anesthesia in surgical patients and (3) is given in doses far exceeding what is needed to keep the inmate from being aware or feeling anything.

Neither Logic nor Science

Regardless of one's feelings about the death penalty as a moral punishment, as a deterrent or whether it is meted out fairly—this latest objection has neither logic nor science to support it. If it did, it would follow that anesthesiologists and nurse anesthetists in this country have been treating patients "unconstitutionally" for decades.

Some years ago, a similar—and unsuccessful—protest was raised that the drugs given for lethal injection hadn't been approved by the Food and Drug Administration as being "safe and effective." Such logic is every bit as tortured as the current flap over pancuronium bromide.

Periodical Bibliography

The following articles have been selected to supplement the diverse views presented in this chapter.

Robert H. Bork	"Travesty Time Again: In Its Death-Penalty Decision, the Supreme Court Hits a New Low," *National Review*, March 28, 2005.
Richard C. Dieter	"Costs of the Death Penalty and Related Issues," testimony to the New York State Assembly Standing Committees on Codes, Judiciary and Correction, January 25, 2005. www.deathpenaltyinfo.org.
Thomas R. Eddlem	"Ten Anti–Death Penalty Fallacies," *New American*, June 3, 2002.
Ivan Eland	"Ending the Death Penalty for Juveniles Is Not Enough," Independent Institute, March 7, 2005. www.independent.org.
Jeff Gillenkirk	"The Death Penalty: A 1% Nonsolution to Crime," *Los Angeles Times*, January 2, 2004.
Michael J. Hurd	"Long Live the Death Penalty," *Capitalism Magazine*, February 20, 2003. www.capmag.com/article.
Jeffrey M. Jones	"Americans' Views of Death Penalty More Positive This Year," *Gallup News Service*, May 19, 2005.
Patrick Leahy	"Death Penalty Overhaul," testimony to the Senate Judiciary Committee, June 18, 2002. www.judiciary.senate.gov.
Raphael Lewis	"Romney Files Death Penalty Bill; Measure Sets Out Tight Restrictions," *Boston Globe*, April 29, 2005. www.boston.com.
Patrick Rollins	"Death Penalty Review Fair," *America's Intelligence Wire*, April 25, 2003.
Jeff Scullin	"Death Penalty: Is the Price of Justice Too High? States Wonder If the Extreme Punishment Is Worth the Cost," *Ledger*, December 14, 2003.
Dudley Sharp	"Death Penalty and Sentencing Information," ProDeathPenalty.com, October 1, 1997. www.prodeathpenalty.com.
Jean M. Templeton	"Shutting Down Death Row: Illinois' Death-Penalty Reforms May Presage a Fairer Criminal-Justice System," *American Prospect*, July 2004.
Texas Lawyer	"The Death Penalty Process: Correcting the Errors," September 15, 2003.

For Further Discussion

Chapter 1

1. After reading all of the viewpoints in this chapter, do you think that it is possible for the death penalty to be constitutional but not moral? Why or why not?

2. Jeff Jacoby argues that the death penalty protects innocent people while the *Daily Record* Advisory Board argues that the death penalty kills innocent people. After reading these viewpoints, and other viewpoints in the book that address errors in the death penalty system, do you think that the potential execution of an innocent person makes the death penalty unjust in all circumstances? Please explain.

Chapter 2

1. Compare and contrast the commonsense argument that the death penalty deters crime with the econometric argument by Iain Murray. In your opinion, which of the two is more convincing?

2. After reading Marshall Dayan and Ted Goertzel's viewpoints carefully, which type of argument—commonsensical or statistical—do you find more convincing? Explain.

3. In the years after the terrorist attacks of September 11, 2001, lawmakers have passed a series of laws designed to protect Americans against such an attack. After reading the viewpoints by Johnny Sutton and Timothy H. Edgar, consider the effectiveness of the death penalty as a deterrent to terrorism. How effective is it, in your view? Explain your answer, citing Sutton and Edgar's viewpoints to support your stand.

Chapter 3

1. How do Christina Swarns and John Perazzo interpret statistics about the alleged bias against minorities in death penalty trials? What are some reasons for the differences in their interpretation? What does this tell you about the use of statistics to support an argument? Who do you think constructs the more convincing case, and why?

2. The Supreme Court ruled on March 1, 2005, that juveniles could not be subjected to the death penalty. After carefully reading Anthony M. Kennedy's statement of the majority opinion and Sandra Day O'Connor's dissent, which do you find more convincing and why?

3. Richard Dieter and Paul A. Logli as well as other writers in this volume reference DNA evidence. How do death penalty advocates use recent advancements in DNA technology to bolster their claims that the death penalty system can be made error-free? What is the death penalty abolitionist response to these claims?

Chapter 4

1. Many of the writers of the viewpoints in this book cite statistics concerning American support or lack of support for the death penalty. How important is public opinion to the question of whether or not the death penalty should be abolished or reformed? How important is international opinion?

2. The Women's Bar Association of the State of New York and Amnesty International identify what they view as irreparable problems with the death penalty. What are their major concerns? How do Steven D. Stewart and Dudley Sharp respond to such concerns? What reforms to the death penalty might address the concerns of death penalty abolitionists?

3. George Sjostrom and Jon Sorensen discuss the various costs associated with the death penalty. In your opinion, should cost be a factor in the decision to abolish or maintain the death penalty? Cite specifics from the viewpoints while developing your answer.

Organizations to Contact

American Bar Association (ABA)
541 N. Fairbanks Ct., Chicago, IL 60611
(312) 988-5522
Web site: www.abanet.org

The American Bar Association is a voluntary professional association. With more than 400,000 members, the ABA provides law school accreditation, continuing legal education, information about the law, programs to assist lawyers and judges in their work, and initiatives to improve the legal system for the public. Links to the ABA's Juvenile Justice Center and to the ABA Legal Aid and Indigent Defendants Committee are available through the Web site. The organization publishes many useful pamphlets, working papers, and reports, including Gideon's *Broken Promise: America's Continuing Quest for Equal Justice*, available through the mail or online.

American Civil Liberties Union (ACLU)
Capital Punishment Project
125 Broad St., 18th Fl., New York, NY 10004
(212) 549-2500 • fax: (212) 549-2426
Web site: www.aclu.org

The ACLU's Capital Punishment Project is dedicated to abolishing the death penalty. The ACLU believes that capital punishment violates the Constitution's ban on cruel and unusual punishment as well as the requirements of due process and equal protection under the law. It publishes and distributes many books and pamphlets, including *Mental Illness and the Death Penalty in the United States*, *The Death Penalty: Questions and Answers*, and *The Forgotten Population: A Look At Death Row in the United States Through the Experiences of Women*.

Amnesty International USA (AI)
5 Penn Plaza, 14th Fl., New York, NY 10001
(212) 807-8400 • fax: (212) 627-1451
Web site: www.amnestyusa.org

Amnesty International is an independent worldwide movement working for the release of all prisoners of conscience, fair and prompt trials for political prisoners, and an end to torture and executions. AI is funded through donations from its members and supporters throughout the world. AI has published several books and reports, including *Fatal Flaws: Innocence and the Death Penalty*.

Criminal Justice Legal Foundation (CJLF)
PO Box 1199, Sacramento, CA 95812
(916) 446-0345
Web site: www.cjlf.org

The Criminal Justice Legal Foundation is a nonprofit, public interest law organization dedicated to restoring a balance between the rights of crime victims and the criminally accused. The foundation's purpose is to assure that people who are guilty of committing crimes receive swift and certain punishment in an orderly and thoroughly constitutional manner. To accomplish this, CJLF attorneys introduce friend of the court briefs in criminal cases before the state and federal courts of appeals to encourage precedent-setting decisions that recognize the constitutional rights of victims and law-abiding society. The foundation provides many documents concerning the death penalty through its Web site, including *Prosecutors' Perspective on California's Death Penalty*, as well as links to studies on the deterrent effect of the death penalty.

Death Penalty Information Center
1320 Eighteenth St. NW, 5th Fl., Washington, DC 20036
(202) 293-6970 • fax: (202) 822-4787
Web site: www.deathpenaltyinfo.org

The Death Penalty Information Center is a nonprofit organization serving the media and the public with analysis and information on issues concerning capital punishment. The center prepares in-depth reports, issues press releases, conducts briefings for journalists, and serves as an information resource. The center offers many news updates, pamphlets, reports, statistics, and publications such as *Innocence and the Crisis in the American Death Penalty*. It also provides a weekly news update through an e-mail subscription.

Justice Fellowship
44180 Riverside Pkwy., Lansdowne, VA 20176
(800) 217-2743
Web site: www.justicefellowship.org

The Justice Fellowship is a nonprofit online community of Christians working to reform the criminal justice system to reflect biblically based principles of restorative justice. Its many publications include *Dialogue on Capital Punishment* as well as a free newsletter available through its Web site.

Justice for All
PO Box 55159, Houston, TX 77255
(713) 935-9300 • (713) 478-9301
e-mail: info@jfa.net • Web site: www.jfa.net
Justice for All is a not-for-profit criminal justice reform organization that supports the death penalty. Its activities include circulating online petitions to keep violent offenders from being paroled early and publishing the monthly newsletter *The Voice of Justice*. It also maintains the Web sites www.prodeathpenalty.com and www.murdervictims.com. These sites provide up-to-date articles and information.

National Coalition to Abolish the Death Penalty (NCADP)
920 Pennsylvania Ave. SE, Washington, DC 20003
(202) 543-9577 • fax: (202) 543-7798
Web site: www.ncadp.org
The National Coalition to Abolish the Death Penalty is a coalition of more than 115 groups working together to stop executions in the United States. The NCADP compiles statistics on the death penalty. To further its goal, the coalition publishes *Legislative Action to Abolish the Death Penalty*, information packets, pamphlets, and research materials.

National Criminal Justice Reference Service
U.S. Department of Justice
PO Box 6000, Rockville, MD 20849-6000
(301) 519-5500 • (800) 851-3420
e-mail: askncjr@ncjrs.org • Web site: www.ncjrs.org
The National Criminal Justice Reference Service is one of the most extensive sources of information on criminal and juvenile justice in the world. Through its Web site, readers can access the Bureau of Justice Statistics regarding the death penalty. Its publications include *Juveniles and the Death Penalty*.

Pro-Death-Penalty.Org
c/o MC4SE, PO Box 154, Belcamp, MD 21017
e-mail: pdporg@comcast.net • Web site: www.pdporg.org
Pro-Death-Penalty.Org works for murder victims' rights and for the fair application of the death penalty. The organization maintains an extensive Web site with articles, links, and statistical information. In addition, the Web site provides a message-board discussion group and tributes to specific murder victims. The organization's publications include *Death Penalty Facts*.

Bibliography of Books

David Anderson · *Death Penalty: A Defence.* 2005. www.yesdeath penalty.com.

Stuart Banner · *The Death Penalty: An American History.* Cambridge, MA: Harvard University Press, 2002.

Hugo Adam Bedau and Paul G. Cassell · *Debating the Death Penalty: Should America Have Capital Punishment?* New York: Oxford University Press, 2004.

Terry Bergstrom and Amy Pasternak · *Capital Punishment.* Lansing, MI: Legislative Research Division, Legislative Service Bureau, 2002.

John D. Bessler · *Kiss of Death: America's Love Affair with the Death Penalty.* Boston: Northeastern University Press, 2003.

Robert M. Bohm · *Deathquest II: An Introduction to the Theory and Practice of Capital Punishment in the United States.* Cincinnati, OH: Anderson, 2003.

Christian E. Brugger · *Capital Punishment and Roman Catholic Moral Tradition.* Notre Dame, IN: University of Notre Dame Press, 2003.

Stanley Cohen · *The Wrong Men: America's Epidemic of Wrongful Death Row Convictions.* New York: Carroll & Graf, 2003.

Randall Coyne · *Capital Punishment and the Judicial Process.* Durham, NC: Carolina Academic Press, 2001.

David R. Dow and Mark Dow, eds. · *Machinery of Death: The Reality of America's Death Penalty Regime.* New York: Routledge, 2002.

Kellie Dworaczyk · *Should Juvenile Offenders Receive the Death Penalty?* Austin: House Research Organization, Texas House of Representatives, 2002.

Michael Foley · *Arbitrary and Capricious: The Supreme Court, the Constitution, and the Death Penalty.* Westport, CT: Praeger, 2003.

Marvin D. Free · *Racial Issues in Criminal Justice: The Case of African Americans.* Westport, CT: Praeger, 2003.

Mark Fuhrman · *Death and Justice: An Exposé of Oklahoma's Death Row Machine.* New York: Morrow, 2003.

John F. Galliher, Larry W. Koch, David Patrick Keyes, and Teresa J. Guess · *America Without the Death Penalty: States Leading the Way.* Boston: Northeastern University Press, 2002.

Stephen P. Garvey	*Beyond Repair? America's Death Penalty.* Durham, NC: Duke University Press, 2003.
Gary P. Gershman	*Death Penalty on Trial: A Handbook with Cases, Laws, and Documents.* Santa Barbara, CA: ABC-CLIO, 2005.
L. Kay Gillespie	*Inside the Death Chamber: Exploring Executions.* Boston: Allyn and Bacon, 2003.
Raphael Goldman and Ann Chih Lin	*Capital Punishment.* Washington, DC: CQ Press, 2001.
Mike Gray	*The Death Game: Capital Punishment and the Luck of the Draw.* Monroe, ME: Common Courage Press, 2003.
Gardner C. Hanks	*Capital Punishment and the Bible.* Scottdale, PA: Herald Press, 2002.
Maureen Harrison	*Death Penalty Decisions of the United States Supreme Court.* Carlsbad, CA: Excellent Books, 2003.
Maurene J. Hinds	*Furman v. Georgia and the Death Penalty Debate: Debating Supreme Court Decisions.* Berkeley Heights, NJ: Enslow, 2005.
Roger G. Hood	*The Death Penalty: A World Wide Perspective.* New York: Oxford University Press, 2002.
Jesse Jackson, Jesse Jackson Jr., and Bruce Shapiro	*Legal Lynching: The Death Penalty and America's Future.* New York: W.W. Norton, 2001.
Judith W. Kay	*Murdering Myths: The Story Behind the Death Penalty.* Lanham, MD: Rowman and Littlefield, 2005.
Michael Kerrigan	*Death Row and Capital Punishment.* Broomall, PA: Mason Crest, 2005.
Rachel King	*Broken Justice: The Death Penalty in Virginia.* Richmond, VA: American Civil Liberties Union of Virginia, 2003.
Michael Kronenwetter	*Capital Punishment: A Reference Handbook.* Santa Barbara, CA: ABC-CLIO, 2001.
Bill Kurtis	*The Death Penalty on Trial: Crisis in American Justice.* New York: Public Affairs, 2004.
Harvey W. Kushner, ed.	*Essential Readings on Political Terrorism: Analyses of Problems and Prospects for the 21st Century.* Lincoln: University of Nebraska Press, 2002.
Barry Latzer	*Death Penalty Cases: Leading U.S. Supreme Court Cases on Capital Punishment.* Boston: Butterworth-Heinemann, 2002.

Joseph L. Lentol and
Jeffrion L. Aubry

Public Hearing on the Death Penalty: New York State Legislature, Assembly, Standing Committee on Codes. New York: EN-DE Reporting Services, 2005.

Robert Jay Lifton
and Greg Mitchell

Who Owns Death?: Capital Punishment, the American Conscience, and the End of Executions. New York: Morrow, 2000.

Hunter P. Mabry

Capital Punishment: A Faith-Based Study. Nashville: Abingdon Press, 2002.

A.V. Mandel

Capital Punishment: Issues and Perspectives. New York: Nova Science, 2002.

Evan J. Mandery

Capital Punishment: A Balanced Examination. Sudbury, MA: Jones and Bartlett, 2005.

Christopher D.
Marshall

Beyond Retribution: A New Testament Vision for Justice, Crime and Punishment. Grand Rapids, MI: William B. Eerdmans, 2001.

J. Michael Martinez,
William D.
Richardson,
D. Brandon
Hornsby, eds.

The Leviathan's Choice: Capital Punishment in the Twenty-First Century. Lanham, MD: Rowman and Littlefield, 2002.

Michael Mello

Deathwork: Defending the Condemned. Minneapolis: University of Minnesota Press, 2002.

Lane Nelson and
Burke Foster

Death Watch: A Death Penalty Anthology. Upper Saddle River, NJ: Prentice Hall, 2001.

Erik C. Owens,
John D. Carlson, and
Eric P. Elshtain, eds.

Religion and the Death Penalty: A Call for Reckoning. Grand Rapids, MI: W.B. Eerdmans, 2004.

Louis J. Palmer

Encyclopedia of Capital Punishment in the United States. Jefferson, NC: McFarland, 2001.

Helen Prejean

The Death of Innocents: An Eyewitness Account of Wrongful Executions. New York: Random House, 2005.

Dale S. Recinella

The Biblical Truth About America's Death Penalty. Boston: Northeastern University Press, 2005.

Mei Ling Rein

Capital Punishment: Cruel and Unusual? Detroit: Gale Group, 2000.

Albert R. Roberts

Critical Issues in Crime and Justice. Thousand Oaks, CA: Sage, 2003.

Roxanne Rodriguez

The Modern Death Penalty: A Legal Research Guide. Buffalo, NY: W.S. Hein, 2001.

Austin Sarat

The Death Penalty: Influences and Outcomes. Burlington VT: Ashgate, 2005.

Austin Sarat	*When the State Kills: Capital Punishment and the American Condition.* Princeton: Princeton University Press, 2001.
Susan F. Sharp	*Hidden Victims: The Effects of the Death Penalty on Families of the Accused.* New Brunswick, NJ: Rutgers University Press, 2005.
Ivan Solotaroff	*The Last Face You'll Ever See: The Private Life of the American Death Penalty.* New York: HarperCollins, 2001.
Eliza Steelwater	*The Hangman's Knot: Lynching, Legal Execution, and America's Struggle with the Death Penalty.* Boulder, CO: Westview Press, 2003.
Victor L. Streib	*Death Penalty: In a Nutshell.* St. Paul, MN: Thomson/West, 2003.
Thomas Streissguth	*The Death Penalty: Debating Capital Punishment.* Berkeley Heights, NJ: Enslow, 2002.
Scott E. Sundby	*A Life and Death Decision: A Jury Weighs the Death Penalty.* New York: Palgrave Macmillan, 2005.
Scott Turow	*Ultimate Punishment: A Lawyer's Reflections on Dealing with the Death Penalty.* New York: Farrar, Straus and Giroux, 2003.
Michael L. Varnado	*Victims of Dead Man Walking.* Gretna, LA: Pelican, 2003.
Saundra Davis Westervelt and John A. Humphrey	*Wrongly Convicted: Perspectives on Failed Justice.* New Brusnwick, NJ: Rutgers University Press, 2001.
Franklin E. Zimring	*The Contradictions of American Capital Punishment.* New York: Oxford University Press, 2003.
Aharon W. Zorea	*In the Image of God: A Christian Response to Capital Punishment.* Lanham, MD: University Press of America, 2000.

Index